Female Energy Awakening

The path of the Worldwide W̶ ... ing
back to Authen...

"I would like to thank ... Womb
Blessing has introduced in n̶ ... COs early
last year and was therefore una... ...elieve the Womb
Blessing healed me, and as a res ... ...y girl was conceived on
the night of the October Womb ...

VB, United Kingdom

"I have done a lot of other spiritual work the last 30 years of my life, since I have always been open, but this work is one of the most powerful. It makes me come home into the deepest parts of myself and I feel that every time I give a Personal Womb Blessing, it is getting deeper and deeper. Thank you so much! I feel such deep gratitude."

SB, Norway

"To live in a time when we have access to a forum of which women from all over the world can circle around and discuss our Divine Feminine essences, our moon cycles, and give and receive Womb Blessings and Healings is a sheer miracle."

JMH, USA

"I would like to thank you for the Womb Blessing received in May. A beloved friend of mine introduced me to this special opportunity that you give to all the women. During the meditation, I felt a lot of energy. The miracle is that I found myself pregnant, after 15 days. I call it miracle, because I didn't believe any more that I could become a mother, so this appears to me as an unexpected surprise and a pure blessing."

FS, Spain

"The Womb Blessing has been so powerful. So immensely rewarding. Never have I felt so held and cherished in the presence of so many souls."

MA, Switzerland

"I think I've said many times, but I want to say a huge THANK YOU! My life has been transformed and illuminated with Womb Blessing."

US, Argentina

"The more I practise living attuned with the changes of my cyclic nature, the more balanced I am. It is like the more I change, the more I am the same."

VC, Costa Rica

"The Womb Blessing has transformed me. Now I am a secure woman. The Womb Blessing has shown me my security and my gifts and has really healed my body, my spiritual soul, my heart and my family!"

LV, Italy

"Miranda has an understanding of the Divine Feminine that not only channels the symbolic beauty of welcoming the feminine archetypes into your life, but she has an intimate understanding of the technical aspects that are involved when people start on a path of personal spiritual practice and the questions that may arise with such an endeavour. The sweetness with which she answers these questions and insecurities and guides you through the process of re-learning your true nature as a woman, are full of grace and loving care."

BMKL, Switzerland

"I have embraced my feminine power and discovered unclaimed gifts of healing. I am able to give and receive pleasure. I also feel more open in my womb area and I view my body as beautiful—a holy temple and treat it with love, acceptance, compassion, and respect."

A, Canada

"Once per year we create a big Worldwide Womb Blessing event in a public park in Bogota with more than 200 people!"

AY, Colombia

"I feel a deeper wisdom inside of me, and all my fears and worries regarding pregnancy, birth and motherhood disappeared... I feel that the Womb Blessing is, for women, that subtle touch which makes it all better, whole. So I really, really thank you for starting this Womb Blessing movement, it is so important because I can see it changes women inside for the better."

MP, Croatia

www.wombblessing.com

Female Energy Awakening

*The path of the Worldwide Womb Blessing
back to Authentic Femininity*

MIRANDA GRAY

Dance your path and awaken!

For

Miranda

2016

Dancing
Eve

http://www.fast-print.net/bookshop

FEMALE ENERGY AWAKENING
THE PATH OF THE WORLDWIDE WOMB BLESSING BACK TO AUTHENTIC FEMININITY
Copyright © Miranda Gray & Richard Gray 2016

ISBN 978-178456-278-6

First Published 2016 by
Fast-Print Publishing of Peterborough, England.

Contents

To all women worldwide who hear a cry in their hearts to awaken, to heal, and to change the world.

Author's note

I write this note after teaching in Mexico, as we take off from Mexico City and fly over the ancient pyramids of Teotihuacan. Earlier in the week I had climbed the Pyramid of the Moon and looked down at the processional way of the Avenue of the Dead stretching out before me and at the large Pyramid of the Sun to the left. Before me, the landscape rose in softly swelling hills; but I no longer saw just the hills, but the form of a reclining woman, her belly in front of me, her breasts in the distance and her up-drawn knees either side. As the tourist parties in their bright colours started to flock down the processional way towards me in the growing heat, I saw the children of the 'Goddess of the Land' being born into the world from between her legs and beneath her belly. I stood seeing what the ancient pre-Colombian inhabitants saw from atop the pyramid – the Sacred Feminine giving birth to her children. I wondered how many tourists realised that they were an active part of an ancient and sacred enactment!

The Sacred Feminine has always been with us, sometimes acknowledged, loved and celebrated, and at other times repressed, vilified, hidden or ignored. But She has always been there in the landscape and within women – we only have to shift how we see things to acknowledge Her presence.

This book is based on the Worldwide Womb Blessing, but you do not need to have taken part to have wonderful experiences and awakening insights with the meditations, information and exercises contained here. However, I hope that you hear the call in your heart to experience the Womb Blessing and to share with your friends the invitation to join with many thousands of women across the globe in the Worldwide Womb Blessing meditation.

If you haven't already experienced the Worldwide Womb Blessing, or if you have registered before and now wish to journey deeper into your authentic female nature, register for the next Blessing – go to www.wombblessing.com and click on the *'register now'* link.

You do not need a physical womb or a menstrual cycle to take part in the Womb Blessing or to do the meditations and exercises in this book. You will still feel the gifts and benefits.

Miranda Gray

Introduction: Our authentic femininity

Our *authentic femininity* is the 'original' femininity we are born with. It lies in our female body, in our cells, in our bones, in our DNA, in our instinctual self and our deepest patterns of behaviour. It is who we are before the modern world takes over with all the restrictions and expectations of our upbringing and society.

We can think of our femininity as being like an old masterpiece painting that has become dirty and darkened with time. We can see the rough shape of the painting underneath the layers of dirt, but we cannot see the beauty of the original colours or the intricacies and details of the true picture. For so many of us we are living a faint outline of our original femininity.

The Womb Blessing cleans away the dirt and restrictions on our femininity. With each Blessing, the layers of dirt become thinner, and we begin to see the original colours shine through. Eventually the whole picture is clean, and we see the beauty of the original masterpiece – the vibrancy and fluidity of the artist's colours and lines, the detail and subtleness and the contrast and emotion of the painting are revealed in all their glory. We feel that we have come home to the beauty and vibrancy of who we truly are. We feel whole and centred, empowered and free, worthy, creative, sexual and spiritual. And we are free to be everything – every colour and every shape of our original femininity.

The painter of our masterpiece is the Sacred Feminine and, like every artist, She puts Her heart, Her soul, and Her energies into the painting – energies that are uniquely female because they express and reflect Her nature. These energies flow through our being and through our levels of awareness. They flow through our core patterns and through the principal female energy centres within our body. For many of us these energies are hidden beneath the dark layers of restriction, but sometimes we see their bright colours appear in our lives and they cause confusion and disruption because we can't see the whole picture. The Womb Blessings helps us to reconnect with these energies within us – to accept and love them as they gradually awaken in our lives, and to live in harmony with them so that we don't return to the darkness.

When modern life tries to bury our colours, the Womb Blessing clears away the dirt and returns our vibrancy to us.

The first Worldwide Womb Blessing was offered on the full moon of February 2012, and it started, as many ideas do, with an open heart and a desire to help. The initial hope for reaching and helping fifty women grew throughout 2012 into a worldwide female spiritual movement reaching thousands of women around the globe.

What started in 2012 has not stopped, but like a bud it has blossomed into something beautiful. Just as the moon flows from crescent to full, from full to crescent, and crescent to hidden; just as a bud opens to flower, then fruits; and just as the maiden matures, becomes a mother, a wise woman, and an elderly woman – our awakening has a cycle to it.

What is the Womb Blessing?

The full title of the Womb Blessing is the 'Womb Blessing Attunement – Female Energy Awakening'. We call it the 'Womb Blessing' or the 'Blessing' for simplicity. An *attunement* is an energy technique that raises an individual's vibration to align with and connect to a specific vibration of energy.

The Womb Blessing attunement is specifically designed for the unique energy structure of women, to raise their vibration and connect them to a beautiful vibration of Sacred Feminine love and light – sometimes called the 'Blessing energy'. The effect of the attunement is a transformational process of healing and awakening our female energies. We call this process 'birthing'.

The Womb Blessing is **a personal and spiritual healing and development system** available for all women, regardless of their background, physical condition or beliefs. Our femininity is not just about fertility, or even about having a physical womb or cycle, it is about the original femininity that lies in all women and the energy centre that rests over the womb area. We don't have to **believe** in the authentic femininity of the Sacred Feminine – we **are** it.

The Womb Blessing is an approach – **a way of living everyday life** that brings self-empowerment through understanding our authentic femininity, and that builds confidence within ourselves.

The Womb Blessing has also grown into **a worldwide community of women** who share the need – in their heart, in their womb and in their bones – for the rediscovery and re-awakening of what it means to be female. It is a community that shares experiences, creates female-centric projects, focuses on female healing and development, and supports and validates all women in a non-competitive environment. It is a community that is organic in structure and which grows in response to the needs of women.

Finally, the Womb Blessing is **a shared vision** – of living an authentic female life in a society that supports our female energies. It means pioneering new female-based ways of living, working, and structuring relationships between individual women and groups of women. It means changing traditional, societal, educational, and work structures and expectations to create a legacy for our daughters and granddaughters so that they may grow up and thrive in a world that welcomes and encourages the full range of female energies and abilities.

Through the beautiful meditations and exercises in this book, and through taking part in the Worldwide Womb Blessings, you will open to your authentic femininity, start a process of self- healing, and begin to create a personal relationship with the Sacred Feminine. The world will start to change for you, for your partner, for your children and for the future – for the better.

It is my heartfelt hope that the Womb Blessing will grow, reaching women far and wide and offering them the safe and supportive family that their souls call for. Whether you are alone in your heartache for connection with your femininity and the Sacred Feminine, whether you are new to Her presence, or whether She has been part of your life and circle of friends for many years, we are all part of a single image of sacred and authentic femininity. Now, perhaps, is the time for us to consciously join together to awaken our feminine energies and to do things in a 'feminine' way – and then we will see what authentic femininity creates.

Big changes are often made by small groups of inspired people – I hope that this book will inspire you.

**Each Womb Blessing
is a gift of Sacred Feminine energy**
that awakens aspects of our authentic femininity
from their sleep, restriction and darkness
and
reveals the beauty,
strength and gifts
of our female nature.

**Each Blessing ignites
the mystery within us**
that is the Sacred Feminine,
and
takes us on a path
that returns us
to our true and sacred
authentic female nature.

Each Blessing brings
healing and acceptance,
love and joy,
guidance and empowerment.

The Sacred Feminine
is reflected in all women
whatever their age,
whatever they do,
with or without a womb,
with or without a menstrual cycle.

The Womb Blessing Meditation

Close your eyes and bring your awareness into your body.

Feel your weight on the cushion, the weight of your arms in your lap. Take a deep breath and feel centred within.

Bring your awareness to your womb; see, know, feel or imagine that your womb is like a tree, with two main branches and beautiful leaves and red, jewel-like fruits on the end.

Feel or imagine that the roots of the tree grow down deep within the darkness of the earth, connecting you and anchoring you, allowing you to receive golden energy into your womb.

Feel grounded and balanced. (Pause)

Now allow the image of your Womb Tree to grow until the tree's branches separate at the level of your heart.

As you connect with this image, see or feel your heart centre open and energy flow down your arms into your hands and fingers.

Feel the connection of love between the earth, your womb and your heart. (Pause)

Still in awareness of your heart, look up and see or feel that the tree's branches continue to reach upwards to cradle a full moon above your head. The beauty of the full moon bathes you in a pure silver-white light that washes through your aura and over your skin. (Pause)

Open to receive the light of the moon. Allow it to enter through your crown and fill your brain with light. (Pause)

Relax further, and receive this light into your heart. (Pause)

Relax even further, open your womb and allow this energy into your womb in blessing. (Pause)

To end the meditation:

Bring your awareness to your Womb Tree roots and feel or know that they grow deep within the earth.

Wiggle your fingers and toes.

Take a deep breath. Open your eyes and smile.

Then have something wonderful to eat!

FEMALE ENERGY AWAKENING

THE PATH OF THE WORLDWIDE WOMB BLESSING
BACK TO AUTHENTIC FEMININITY

The Making of the World

At the making of the world, First Woman opened her eyes and looked around at the trees and the sky, at the river and the mountains, and she asked the first words: 'Who am I?'

And the First Animals of the world responded, and they came to tell her. Hare Woman came forward and gave First Woman a flower.

'You are Hare' she said.

Then Horse Woman left her herd and gave First Woman a mirror.

'You are Horse' she said.

Owl Woman swooped in, dropping a curved knife at First Woman's feet.

'You are Owl' she cried.

And Bear Woman sat in front of First Woman and gave her an obsidian bowl.

'You are Bear' she growled.

First Woman looked at the animals, puzzled, and asked: 'But how can I be all of you?'

So Serpent Woman came up to First Woman and placed a belt around her hips. She attached each object to the belt.

'You are Serpent.' she said, 'You flow'.

Moon Mother suddenly appeared, bathing them all in her beauty and light.

'Ah, First Daughter, you have discovered who you are' she said, smiling.

First Woman looked at her belt, then looked up at Moon Mother.

'But how will I know when I am Hare Clan, Horse Clan, Owl Clan or Bear Clan?' she asked.

Moon Mother replied 'I will show you from the sky. Watch my face grow and be with the Hare people, see my full smile and be with Horse clan, see my face incline and be with the Owl people and then, when I leave the sky, follow me and hibernate with the Bear Clan'.

And First Woman knew who she was.

Chapter 1: The Worldwide Womb Blessing: A personal journey

It's difficult to pinpoint 'the beginning' of the Worldwide Womb Blessing, because so many of my previous experiences and learning came together to create it. The Sacred Feminine has always been part of my path, and even as a child of ten years old I was painting images of goddesses and priestesses. For me there was no distinction between my spirituality and the creative energies that flowed through me. The world around me was sacred, full of energies and inspiration. As someone who thinks in images and feelings it was difficult to find the words to define my experiences, but I knew that expressing my creativity was a beautiful relationship with the divine in the world around me and within me.

In my twenties I wrote my first book, *'Red Moon: Understanding and using the gifts of the menstrual cycle'*, which evolved from my inner cry to know who I was and why I found it so hard to be female in a masculine world. Like First Woman, I asked 'Who am I?'

I was very aware of the changing energies within myself, but without any structure or language to understand these changes I felt that there must be something wrong with me. This was in the days before the widespread availability of knowledge and resources via the internet, so it was not easy to find information about women's energies, healing and spirituality.

I started to share my cycle observations with other women, and found that I was not alone in my experiences. I knew that my observations couldn't just be a modern discovery, that women in the past would have known about these energy changes, and so I explored European mythology and folklore for the ancient female oral wisdom lying within it. Within this mythology I found stories of the Sacred Feminine and the answer to what it means to be female.

Red Moon was the result of my journey of self-discovery. After *Red Moon* was published, I began to teach workshops based on the book and to study alternative healing, energy and spiritual approaches – while at

3

the same time working as a freelance illustrator. I explored Celtic and Western spiritual systems, trained in different forms of energy work including Reiki and in the Flower of Life, and worked as a healer and energy-teacher for sixteen years, alongside being a graphic designer and multimedia developer. As my personal awareness of energy grew, my creativity and inspiration changed from being expressed primarily through artwork to being expressed through spiritual energetic work, and I blended and created new systems based on the energies and inspiration that flowed through me.

At the turn of the millennium something changed – women were no longer interested in understanding their femininity or exploring their connection with the Sacred Feminine, and it took years for the interest to slowly re-awaken. I first saw the green shoots of change in a renewed interest in *Red Moon* and the increasing number of requests for it to be published in different languages. In support of the book, I travelled to different European countries to teach one-day Red Moon workshops. The women I met wanted to know more about their femininity, they wanted to understand themselves, to discover their female energies, and to experience a personal relationship with the Sacred Feminine.

In December 2011 a wonderful friend of mine, Belinda Garcia Reyes, offered to organise a Red Moon workshop for me in London. I asked her what she thought women would like as an addition to the workshop and she suggested that I give a hands-on womb healing to each woman. Sadly the workshop didn't go ahead, but her suggestion started me thinking – and that is always dangerous!

I felt drawn to reach more women than would be possible through small workshops, and I felt called in my heart to offer more than healing. My heart desired that I help women to awaken fully to their authentic femininity and spirituality so that they could live whole, fulfilled and better lives.

For me, all the different forms of my creativity have been the ways in which I hold and share the energy and presence of the Sacred Feminine. Her presence accompanies me and takes form by flowing through me. By following Her energies in my body and by listening to Her voice in Nature and in the stars, in my heart and in my womb and in the earth, the energy work that is the Womb Blessing was born.

I received the first Womb Blessing through a version of a meditation that originated in *Red Moon* and which had then evolved over the years into my personal practice. The beauty of the energy of the first Blessing was breath-taking and started a path of deep transformation which has profoundly changed my life. Each time I prepared to receive the Womb Blessing, I used the meditation to open my energies, to connect with the Sacred Feminine, and to allow Her energy to flow into me and through me. This meditation is now used as the way for all women to prepare to receive the Womb Blessing.

In my heart I knew that this vibration of Sacred Feminine energy was for all women, and not just for those I could meet in person. So, guided by the love of the Sacred Feminine and shaped by my awareness of the Blessing energy and knowledge of energy techniques, the distant Worldwide Womb Blessing took form.

Blessing our femininity: Why the 'womb' and why a 'blessing'?

The word 'womb' in the Womb Blessing is **symbolic** of the original femininity we embody, and of the female energy centre that lies over our lower belly and womb. Whether we have a physical womb or not, we still have this energy centre, and its energies affect all aspects of our lives – the way we think and feel, our sexual energies, our creativity, and our spirituality. We may stop being fertile, but we don't stop embodying a beautiful, magical and empowered femininity.

I chose the term 'blessing' because a blessing is an action that takes something that is seen as ordinary and returns it back to its original sacred nature. A blessing helps us to recognise the divine presence within ourselves and within the world around us. So many women see their womb and its cycles as mundane and with little relevance to their lives – unless they want a child, or their womb causes pain and disruption. Many women hate their cycles, their femininity and their bodies, and are disconnected from the core sacredness and flowing energies that lie within their womb energy centre. The Womb Blessing is a return to sacredness of *everything* that it means to be a female.

The word 'blessing' has many roots in different languages. From the Latin root, the word 'benediction' means to 'speak well of', so a 'womb blessing' is to express into the world the positive aspects of our female energies. In Old English, 'blessing' comes from a word that means to make sacred, especially through blood.

The Womb Blessings are:

A path of return to the original sacredness (symbolised by the word 'blessing') of everything that it means to be female (symbolised by the 'womb'), in a loving embrace. Within this return and loving embrace we know our true self and find empowerment and healing.

The first invitation

In January 2012 I decided to offer the first Worldwide Womb Blessing. I sent out an email invitation to 20 female friends in different countries, inviting them to join me and to pass on the invitation to any women who may be interested. I offered the Womb Blessing at four times during the day to make it accessible to women in different time zones.

Authentic femininity is about connection, weaving patterns, creation, including others, and sharing from our heart. The specific vibration of Sacred Feminine energy in the Worldwide Womb Blessing attunement is not something we are given to hold on to, but something for us to share – so I wrote an additional 'Sharing Meditation'. This meditation enabled all the women taking part to share the energy of the Sacred Feminine with each other through a womb-to-womb link at their chosen time.

I had no idea what was going to happen!

I was delighted when the first registrations started to arrive, but then the emails started to flood in, in their hundreds! I took three weeks away from work, and my husband also had to help me with processing the registrations. In the last few days before the first Worldwide Womb Blessing we were receiving a thousand emails a day, and they came from all over the world – and we were registering them each individually.

The first Worldwide Womb Blessing was given on the full moon nearest to the Celtic festival of Imbolc – or Candlemas in the early calendar. This full moon, at a time when renewal and growth was appearing in the land, resonated deeply with the awakening and activation of our sacred femininity and its emerging growth into the world.

6,029 women took part from over 80 countries.

I was shocked, amazed and deeply honoured. The Sacred Feminine had called, and the hearts and wombs of women were responding to Her.

For me, what started out as a lone activity and a desire to send the Womb Blessing to women around the world became a family of women, connected and interconnected, sending the energy of the Sacred Feminine to each other.

The response to the first Worldwide Womb Blessing

The response to the first Womb Blessing – as shown by the number of registrations, emails, Facebook comments, photographs and testimonials – showed me that one Worldwide Womb Blessing was not enough. The response to the Blessing was a cry from the hearts of women that cut across countries and languages, cultures and spirituality. I cried reading the personal stories emailed to me that showed the depth of strength and courage women hold in the most appalling conditions, situations and life experiences. In these women's voices I felt the strength of the Sacred Feminine, but I also heard the underlying ache of a broken relationship with Her.

Women took part from isolated areas such as the Galapagos Islands, the islands of Réunion and Polynesia, from Arab countries and Israel, from Latin American, North America, Bali, Korea, European countries, Australia and India – to name just a few of the 80 countries represented. Something was connecting these women, and something in their hearts was responding to the simple invitation to take part in a Womb Blessing. That 'something' was a global need to reconnect with the sacredness of our femininity and to validate our strength, creativity, sexuality and spirituality **as women**.

Through a simple Womb Blessing, we had reached far beyond our personal awakening, and had become part of a much wider activation - the awakening of all women, and the awakening of the Sacred Feminine throughout the world. In my heart the Sacred Feminine and the cry of women asked for more global Blessings.

There are now five Worldwide Womb Blessings per year, each one on the full moon closest to one of the Celtic festivals to reflect the energies of the Sacred Feminine as She manifests in the moon's light and in the cycle of the earth. The final Blessing of each year is on the full moon closest to the winter solstice, and is an opportunity for us to connect as a circle of loving sisters who offer healing for the women of the world.

The Worldwide Womb Blessing speaks with the voice of the Sacred Feminine, and she speaks in many languages. It is very important to me that the Blessing is accessible to all women and it is through the great kindness of volunteer translators that the invitation to take part has reached so many women. My initial invitation was the spark, but it is the translators who were the kindling that helped the flames to catch and spread across the world. I cannot thank these women enough for their contribution – without them we would not have the Womb Blessing in over 150 countries around the world.

The birth of 'Moon Mothers'

The Blessing has always been about sharing the awakening of women to their authentic femininity. It has grown and evolved in an organic female way – unstructured, creative, intuitive, inspired and responsive. After the first Womb Blessing Day, many women contacted me asking to learn how to give the Blessing, and in their requests I once again heard the voice of the Sacred Feminine. I committed to follow where She called me, to flow with Her energy and to respond to the requests of women. I knew that the Sacred Feminine was calling these women to spread Her energy to more women through giving individual Womb Blessing attunements, calling them to take part in the service of giving the Blessing vibration of Sacred Feminine energy in the worldwide events, and She was asking them to support women on the path of personal and spiritual development between the Worldwide Womb Blessings.

The Personal Womb Blessing attunement developed out of the Worldwide Womb Blessing, but its effects are slightly different. The Worldwide Womb Blessing works with the common patterns that *the group* at each chosen time needs to clear, but the Personal Womb Blessing focuses solely on the patterns that an *individual* woman most needs to awaken and heal. Both types of Blessing attunement bring transformational awakening, and healing arises from the energy changes.

The first Womb Blessing training workshop was given in London in April 2012, and it initiated a new path for me and for the women who came. We became the first 'Moon Mothers' – women who offered to nurture, support and spread the awakening of women's authentic femininity. The following Worldwide Womb Blessing with the new Moon Mothers taking part was a beautiful and powerful experience. On the womb-link network criss-crossing the earth I saw bright stars – each one a Moon Mother grounding the Sacred Feminine energy in her land and sending the energy through the connecting wombs of all the women talking part.

Moon Mothers: Women wanting to help women

As more women took part in the worldwide events I started to receive invitations to teach in different countries. Each invitation was the voice of the Sacred Feminine showing me where to take the Womb Blessing, and each Moon Mother was a way for the Womb Blessing to reach more women.

The commitment women make to take the training is truly inspiring. For the first workshops women drove across their country at night with their children asleep in the car to get to the workshop. They flew to Europe from Canada, Australia, Mexico and Peru, and many had large financial challenges. It was very humbling to meet all these women, and it showed me the strength of the call in their heart, and their courage and passion. I felt that if women showed this level of commitment to the Sacred Feminine by travelling to learn, then I too needed to show my commitment by travelling the world to teach.

Moon Mothers range in age from 18 to over 80 years old, and although they come from many different backgrounds and have different levels of experience, they all have two things in common – the call of the Sacred Feminine in their heart and the enthusiasm, commitment and love to share the Womb Blessing. In the sharing of the Womb Blessing these women walk a path of intense and powerful personal and spiritual development. In each Blessing they give, they also receive the Blessing themselves and awaken more deeply to their authentic femininity and to the Sacred Feminine. They are pathfinders, women who energetically lead the way so that other women can follow, and they are women who increasingly hold more of the vibration of authentic femininity so that other women will resonate in response.

Moon Mothers and Female Energy Balancing

Most women find that the path of awakening at each Blessing is full of joy, connection and soulfulness, but for some their birthing process can be a little more physical and emotionally intense. To help these women through their birthing I taught Moon Mothers a *Womb Healing – Female Energy Balancing* focusing on the three main female energy centres and on balancing and restoring energy to blocked or depleted aspects of women's energies. As this Healing developed it also became used to help women to prepare for the Worldwide Womb Blessing, to support young girls as they enter womanhood, and to help women with their menstrual cycle and physical difficulties.

Female Energy Balancing is also used to support women during peri-menopause and in post-menopause. Peri-menopause is the time when women's cycles begin to become irregular, and post-menopause is the time after their last menstruation. The early stages of post-menopause can be as challenging as peri-menopause because women are still going through many changes.

Worldwide Womb Blessing groups

The call of the Sacred Feminine is a strong driving force in the growth and development of the Womb Blessing. Many women around the world felt Her call to connect and share with each other, and Worldwide Womb Blessing groups started to appear in different countries independently. Some groups were small and private, consisting of a few friends and family members, others were large and public consisting of over a hundred women. Groups also connected across countries through Skype or via web conferencing software to participate in the meditations together.

The Worldwide Womb Blessing has become a beautiful celebration, as well as a blessing of everything that it means to be female. It has inspired some to meet together, especially in parts of the world where women thought they were alone in their heart's call and experiences. For women who do not have a local group, or who live in a regime where they cannot openly express their authentic femininity, the worldwide events connect them to a female spiritual family that supports their awakening and validates all aspects of their femininity as good, worthy and beautiful.

The Womb Blessing has spread across the world because women have trusted their hearts and have given generously of their time and talents. My original offering was just the spark, and the fire now belongs to the creative and inspirational women who feed it and gather women together to sit beside it to share their stories, tears, happiness and experiences with each other.

The youngest 'woman' that I know of who has taken part in the Worldwide Womb Blessing is just 9 years old, and the eldest woman is 91. We all have so much light and life, courage and enthusiasm, love and strength that we can offer to each other, whatever our age.

For me, the Womb Blessing journey has been one of huge challenges and changes. Sometimes I step so far outside of my 'comfort zone' that I can't remember what it looks like. The Womb Blessing has always been, and will always be, at the service of the Sacred Feminine for the awakening of women in accordance with Her Love. When women show so much strength and commitment to the call of the Sacred Feminine it is obvious that this awakening is just the start of something amazing and world changing.

Exercise: The Moon Inside: Connecting to the moon within your womb energy centre

This gentle exercise begins a relationship between you and your womb energy centre. It focuses on the pelvic girdle that partially encircles your lower belly and which creates the beautiful bowl to hold a baby as it grows.

The meditation below is a beautiful way to bring your awareness down from your head to your womb energy centre – the centre of your female energies and empowerment. It can also help to reduce the stresses and strains of everyday life. The more attention you give to your womb centre, the more it becomes your source of strength and grounding.

As with all the meditations in this book, *you do not need a physical womb or a menstrual cycle* to do the meditation and to feel the benefits.

Sit comfortably and take a deep breath.

Close your eyes and bring your awareness to your physical womb or the womb energy centre that covers your lower belly.

Take a deep breath into your lower belly and relax.

See, know or feel that a beautiful golden bowl, filled with water, sits in the cradle of your pelvic girdle.

As you look into the bowl you see the reflection of the full moon and stars.

Take another deep breath and relax the muscles of your lower belly.

Now be aware of a full moon above you and the reflection of its light in your womb. See or know that you hold the light of the moon within you.

Notice how you feel.

Notice any physical sensations.

Your womb centre is connected to the cycles and to the beautiful energies and love of the Sacred Feminine.

When you are ready, place your hands on your lower belly. Take a deep breath, open your eyes and smile.

Chapter 2:
Why is the womb so important?

One morning First Woman was sitting by the river, making a pot from the mud. She left it to dry in the sunlight, and the pot was so beautiful that the First Animals came to admire it. By the evening the animals and First Woman were tired and thirsty, so she filled the pot with water from the river and gave each animal their fill. Now the animals were also hungry, and First Woman had nothing to give them, so she called out to Moon Mother as her full face rose in the sky:

'Mother please help. I need food for the First animals. What can I do?'

Moon Mother called down, 'Fill your bowl with my light and I will create enough for everyone'.

First Woman raised the bowl above her head so it could fill with moonlight, and when she lowered it, food of all types flowed from her bowl. The animals came to her and ate until they were so full and sleepy that they curled up around First Woman and slept.

First Woman was also ready to sleep, but she had nowhere to put her bowl. 'Mother' she called, 'I have nowhere to put my bowl. Can you keep it for me please?'

Moon Mother replied 'I will put it somewhere safe for you so that you can use it whenever you have need'.

The bowl transformed into light, and through a single moonbeam Moon Mother placed the bowl in First Woman's lower belly.

'Ah' sighed First Woman, and she went to sleep with her hands over her new bowl.

The modern world's approach to the womb

Disconnection from our full being

The development of modern science and medicine has had an important role in shaping how we feel about our womb.

The masculine approach of objectiveness and 'fixing' things has taken many women away from the subjective experiential awareness of their female energies and prevented the validation of these important experiences. The womb centre, the mind, and the heart are deeply linked, and to work with just the physical is to separate women from their full being and from the full perception of themselves and of life. The result of this isolation of the self is to live from an unconscious fear-based approach.

By removing feelings of wholeness, creativity and empowerment from our lives, and by making natural aspects of ourselves unacceptable and a threat to our survival or status if we do not override them, society triggers our primitive brain response of 'fight or flight'. Our lives then reflect these two responses with episodes where fear, anger and aggression drive us, or anxiety and a sense of vulnerability restrict us. Our primitive survival and stress responses overwhelm the beautiful changes and gifts that lie in the phases of our womb's cycles and alienate us further from the supportive and life-affirming experiences they bring. We lose touch with the joy of a spiritual relationship with the world and the pleasure of unlocking and expressing our inspiration and creative power. Without understanding why we feel disconnected, feelings of frustration, inner turmoil and self-hatred arise, creating unfulfilled lives, physical problems with our wombs and cycles, problems with relationships, and a lack of purpose and direction in life.

In the 1960s and 1970s the introduction of 'The Pill' freed us from the fear of unwanted pregnancies, but it also created in women's minds the science-led approach of controlling and 'fixing' the body and the menstrual cycle. Rather than the freedom 'The Pill' promised women, it has alienated successive generations from their cycles and female energies until many women live in a culture where the effect of their womb and cycles is at best seen as irrelevant and at worst seen as negative.

Science and medicine 'solve' the physical 'problems'. Through subtle (and sometimes not so subtle) advertising, pharmaceutical companies teach women that the centre of female empowerment, the womb, is a problem that can only be fixed by suppression. The actual underlying problem – living in a society that forces us into an unnatural expression of femininity in order to survive – is not addressed, and so women's physical, mental and emotional problems continue to develop and grow.

Reconnecting: Hope and the path forward

We all embody disconnection from our womb to some degree because we have never had the freedom to grow up living totally female lives in a society that validates and nurtures authentic femininity.

The Womb Blessings offer us hope and a new path, not just for ourselves but also for future generations. They offer us healing and release, and a way to return to feeling 'good' about our body and our self again. They provide us with what we ache for in our heart and in our womb – a way to feel authentic, connected and whole in our self.

Exercise: What is disconnection?

Connection is about experiencing a sense of self.

> Take a moment to notice where your sense of self lies within your body.

> The answer could be 'in my head', or if you are feeling loving at the moment, it could be 'in my heart'.

> Now be aware of the palms of your hands. Do you feel them? Are they a part of you? Are they part of your sense of self?

> What about the soles of your feet? Can you feel them? Are they part of you?

> Now bring your awareness to your womb, or womb centre, that lies in your lower belly. Can you feel it? Does it feel part of your sense of self?

For those of us who live 'in our heads' it can be very difficult for us to feel a sense of self in our womb unless we are experiencing pre-menstrual cramping or we are pregnant. This lack of awareness of our womb and the lack of a sense of self lying within our womb is the result of disconnection.

You may have noticed that during this simple exercise your womb has started to respond to your attention. Perhaps you are starting to feel its presence, or perhaps it is cramping a little. Your womb is responding to your attention because it wants to re-establish the natural connection between mind and womb.

Exercise: The Magical Womb: awareness of your womb or your womb centre

Now that we have made the first step to connect to our womb, we can start to build an interactive and loving relationship with it. The following meditation was first published in *Red Moon*, and it started a journey that became the Womb Blessing meditation.

If you do not have a womb, you can still do this meditation as a way to connect with the womb energy centre by imagining your womb and ovaries.

Close your eyes and relax your body.

Bring your awareness to your womb.

See in your mind the central womb with the fallopian tubes on either side and the ovaries on the ends.

Become aware of first one ovary and then the other. You may find that you begin to experience a feeling of tightness or of warmth growing in your ovaries or womb.

Now visualize your womb slowly enlarging, until it envelops your body.

Feel the fallopian tubes reaching out from your shoulders and visualize your arms stretching out like the branches, holding the cluster of eggs like fruit in your hands.

Allow the creative energy of your womb to rise up inside you, along your arms and into your fingers, making them tingle.

Feel completely at one with the image of your womb.

Gradually lower your arms and slowly allow the image of your womb to shrink back to its normal size.

Acknowledge the presence of your womb in your lower belly.

Take a deep breath and open your eyes.

You may feel very peaceful after the exercise, or you may feel the need to use the energy raised to create something.

How did you feel?

> Did you feel your womb and your ovaries respond to your attention? Make a note of your experiences.
>
> You may like to try this meditation in the different phases of your menstrual cycle, or in the different phases of the lunar cycle, to release the energies that are part of your nature at these times.

The womb: The seat of female empowerment

The womb energy centre is *the* centre of strength and empowerment for women. It is our energy gateway to the earth and, when this gateway is open and connected, the graceful energy of Mother Earth flows upwards and fills us with vitality, body-confidence, self-belief, sensuality and interconnectedness with the physical world. We feel whole within our self, centred and calm in oneness with our body and the earth. Womb and heart connect directly and our heart centre opens in resonance with the radiant womb centre, helping us to express and use our strength with love.

The cycles of the womb also have a powerful effect on all aspects of our lives – on our physical, emotional and mental energies, our needs and dreams, our creative energies, our sexuality, spirituality, relationships and work. Whether or not we are conscious of its changing energies there is nothing in our lives that is not affected by our cycles. The Sacred Feminine, and Her pattern lying in our authentic femininity, is in everyone's lives!

Our relationship with the womb centre is interactive, not just through our body and feelings but also through our mind and thoughts. The way we perceive our self, our life and the world around us can have a physical effect on our womb and its cycles, and our womb and its cycles can have an equally profound effect on the way we think.

**Our womb centre and its energies
have a deep and powerful effect
on all aspects of our lives.**

We are used to using 'the head' to describe our thinking self and 'the heart' to describe our loving self, and now we need to reclaim 'the womb' to describe our empowered female self.

Home of the female soul

The womb centre is also the spiritual home of the female soul, our pattern of authentic femininity. It is through our disconnection with our womb centre that we have lost our soul-fullness, the feeling of being whole and complete in who we are. We have also lost contact with the guidance and purpose of our soul, and the feelings of empowerment and lasting inner strength and peace that it offers us.

The womb centre links us to the earth and to the moon, to the material and the spiritual. Joining together body, heart and mind through the spiralling cycle of its changing energies we embody the Sacred Feminine who is the originator of the cycles of the Universe and the Creatrix of life. Through the womb centre we are empowered by the realisation that nothing is ever truly lost, that everything exists within the Universal Womb and its cycles of change and creation.

The power of the womb's cycle: More than just fertility

The womb has much more to offer women than 'just' creating the next generation, or causing pain and disruption in women's lives. If there weren't advantages to women having these cyclic energies, natural selection would have ended them thousands of years ago! So the question we need to ask ourselves is:

'What additional value do our cycles and their associated energies have that makes Mother Nature continue them as part of female nature?'

Perhaps we should also ask ourselves, when experiencing a particularly challenging pre-menstrual or menstrual phase, 'What advantage does this experience and behaviour give me? What is its survival benefit, personal benefit and societal benefit?' – there is one.

What value is there to the menstrual cycle beyond fertility?

The menstrual cycle contains within it two different cycles: a cycle of **renewing physical energy and stamina**, and a cycle of **varying levels of dominant thinking and perception**.

Each of our cycles is a wonderful opportunity to renew and restore our mental, emotional and physical energies. Each month, nature gives us approximately a week of rest where she restores our energies ready for the next cycle. In this resting phase something wonderful happens: we are able to access our body's natural healing ability – but only if we stop, let go to our body's needs, and rest.

Each cycle is also an exciting journey through changing levels of perception. We women are sometimes accused of constantly changing our minds – and it's true, we do! Each phase has a level of awareness that is more dominant, and it is this dominance that colours how we see life. The journey of the cycle is a voyage from the upper rational intellectual mind down into the darkness of our deepest and most profound level of awareness – our soul mind. It is when we let go and allow our soul mind to dominate in our menstrual phase that we access the natural energy and rhythms that we also reach in sleep, and we benefit from the healing that this altered state brings.

The dominant levels of awareness we experience in each cycle are:

1. The **Thinking Mind**. Dominant in the pre-ovulation phase, the phase before the egg is released, and often experienced as heightened levels of rational and positive thinking and mental creativity.
2. The **Feeling Mind**. Dominant in the ovulation phase, the phase where we release an egg, and commonly experienced through heightened feelings and empathy and practical creativity.
3. The **Subconscious Mind**. Dominant in the pre-menstrual phase during the days before bleeding, and often experienced in deep behavioural and emotional patterns and heightened intuition and inspired creativity.
4. The **Soul Mind**. Dominant in the menstrual phase, the phase of bleeding, and experienced when we rest as a deep sense of oneness, connection and spiritual wisdom.

Each cycle is an amazing cycle of personal healing and renewing energy. Each cycle is a cycle of different ways of thinking, of different forms of creativity, of changing sexual energy and of fluid spirituality.

This empowers us with **four potential ways** of solving problems, of innovating change, of approaching tasks, of building a family and of creating the world around us. We are unique in this beautiful and amazing and powerful nature – men do not have a menstrual cycle, and there are no other creatures on earth that have these changing abilities and the opportunity to apply them in the way that human females do.

We women are possibly the most flexible, talented and creative creatures on this planet.

It was from these changing aspects of the feminine that we formed the origins of human culture. Through women's cyclic creativity, awareness and energies came the development of family, relationships and community. We can also thank the female cycle for the development of agriculture, cooking, crafts and trade, teaching, the arts and spirituality.

All these things contributed to original culture and society, and the menstrual cycle has been intimately entwined with the success of humanity as a species.

Menopause: Wombs beyond the cycle

If being female is just about fertility, we should ask the questions:

Why do women survive after their fertile years are over? What benefits does Mother Nature see in *these* women?

The energies of the menstrual cycle do not die when our cycles stop. Instead, they combine to create a new type of woman: a Complete Woman. The passage from Cyclic Woman – a woman with a menstrual cycle – to Complete Woman – a woman who naturally no longer has her cycles – is the passage to a new form of femininity with its own strengths, gifts and wisdom. We change like a caterpillar into a butterfly and enter the third of the four life stages of women. These stages are the young girl, the fertile woman, the non-cyclic woman and the elder woman.

To enter the non-cyclic stage of our lives, we evolve into a different form of human female. With time, this phase also evolves into the stage of the elder woman who faces more towards the spiritual than the outer world. But our changes are gradual, and the expectations of society are that we stay the same if we want to survive and be 'worthy'.

Modern women are offered a frightening image of ageing as a degeneration without social or spiritual status.

Nature, however, sees the advantage of these Complete Women – even if modern culture doesn't. Complete Women bring wisdom and experience. In the change from Cyclic Woman to Complete Woman, nature asks us to embrace all the aspects and energies of our authentic femininity that we have not yet lived so that we can hold them within our self in oneness.

A Complete Woman's awareness of the world is deeper, wider, and focused on future generations rather than on personal goals. Her spirituality and spiritual awareness deepens, creating a connection for society with the Sacred Feminine and Her guidance. She is the hand that holds, the guardian of the past and future, the ancient one and the young one. The creative power of the cycle lies within her womb centre as she retains her sacred blood, ready to manifest her desires and dreams in the world.

Complete Women embody the emotional strength and love of the mother, the dynamic energy of the young girl, the intuition and inspiration of the priestess and the inner calm and piercing wisdom of the elder woman. It's no wonder that nature wants to keep them, and that so many societies have wanted to disempower them.

The womb and its accompanying cycle and energies offer much more than modern culture allows.

Our purpose as women is simple: To be authentically female and to accept, love, enjoy and express the amazing energies and gifts that this brings.

Exercise: Stirring the cauldron: Energising the womb centre

This simple visualisation is a very powerful way to revitalise the energies in your womb centre – and you can do it daily. If you felt disconnected from your womb centre in the previous exercise, then you may need to do this exercise several times before you feel a response or experience a change in your energies and feelings.

This exercise is also used as a preparation for the Worldwide Womb Blessing. The more you are connected to your womb centre, the more you will be able to consciously experience the effect of the Womb Blessing energy.

> Sit on a chair or on the floor, with your arms resting lightly in your lap.
>
> Bring your awareness to your lower belly.
>
> Imagine that a beautiful golden cauldron rests in your pelvic girdle. The cauldron is filled with radiant golden liquid.
>
> Now imagine that you have a large silver spoon with a long handle, and you start to stir the liquid lying in your cauldron.
>
> Make circles and figure of eight shapes in the water with your spoon, first one way and then the other. Stir up the energies of your womb centre!
>
> Do this for about five minutes. Have fun!
>
> Now place your hands over your lower belly for a few minutes and open your awareness to how you feel and what you see or know.
>
> When you are ready to finish, smile and feel gratitude. Then gently wiggle your fingers and toes and open your eyes.
>
> Drink some water and have something nice to eat!

For some women this exercise can create a strong physical response. Womb cramping in particular can be a physical sign of the depth of disconnection with the energies of the womb, and a sign of underlying physical stress caused by living out of balance with their cyclic nature.

If you experience cramping, you may wish to stop the exercise and have a warm bath or place a hot water bottle over your lower belly. See this cramping as a positive sign of the interactive relationship between your mind and your womb, and know that we can use this interaction to build a positive relationship.

For other women this exercise can bring feelings of centeredness and strength, and of being energised and sexy.

Chapter 3:
What is the Sacred Feminine?

One night, First Woman was feeling lonely. All the animals were asleep in their beds at home. So she took out her bowl from her lower belly and looked into it.

At first she saw nothing but the ripples of her breath on the water that filled the bowl. So she stirred the water and looked again. In her bowl she saw her own face, which slowly changed to that of a mature woman and then to an elder woman. Surprised, she leaned closer.

First Woman stirred her bowl again, and this time she saw the First Land covered in winter snow. As she watched, the snows melted into spring and first shoots appeared in bright green on the trees. Gradually the trees changed into the emerald greens of summer, and then the leaves turned into the swirling golds and reds of autumn. Finally the trees lay bare in the darkness of winter.

She stirred the waters again, and she saw in them a crescent moon rising into the night sky becoming full, and then decreasing into darkness.

She stirred again and saw the image of the wheel of the stars rising in the night sky to their peak to drop again below the horizon.

She held her bowl up, looking at it in surprise and wonder. It was such a small thing, but it held the Universe!

Ancient wisdom: Understanding the flow of female energies

In the past, the Sacred Feminine was perceived as the Universe. Her body was everything – animals and birds, the earth and the oceans, and the planets and the stars. Just as our spirit and life force dwell in our body, the spirit and life of the Sacred Feminine dwells within the body of the Universe. There is nothing that is not the Sacred Feminine, She is the one and the many, and everything is part of Her. Just as we have different parts of our body – toes, breasts, eyes, bones etc. – the Sacred Feminine also has multiple parts to Her self. Our body is Her body, and our life force and spirit are Her energy and spirit. This means that there is nothing that is 'impure' or 'dirty'. There is nothing that is not sacred, nothing that is not part of Her. The Sacred Feminine expressed is love, and this love is both active *and* passive, dynamic *and* receptive, stillness *and* movement, and spiritual *and* material.

Our ancient female ancestors recognised the Sacred Feminine in all her forms and expressions in the world and also within themselves. They saw Her change in the cycle of the stars, the cycle of the seasons, the cycle of the moon, the cycle of the tides, the cycle of life and in the cycle of women – always changing but always remaining the same. And they honoured all these aspects of the feminine as both the whole cycle and the individual phases.

Something beautiful lost: The female archetypes

Sadly, in the modern world we have lost the ancient wisdom and understanding of the Sacred Feminine and Her expression through authentic femininity. The term 'femininity' has become limited to passivity and selfless caring, deleting the dynamic and powerful aspects that societies and religions have found threatening.

The concept of femininity also suffered with the development and use of the terms 'inner female' and 'inner male', 'masculine side' and 'feminine side', to describe the nature of men and women. If we are female, we are female whether we are receptive and mothering or aggressive and achieving.

When we see a lioness attacking a threat, we don't say that she is expressing her masculine side – we simply accept that she is expressing her natural female nature. We need to give our own femininity the same acceptance.

To call the dynamic side of our nature 'our masculine side' is to limit our understanding and expression of what it is to be female.

Similarly labelling gentleness in a man as 'female' is also to limit our understanding of masculinity. There is no 'inner masculine' side to our energies, instead our femininity is made up of varying levels and expressions of receptive energies *and* dynamic energies.

In folklore and mythology we have an echo of the ancient understanding of female energies and their cyclic energies in stories about four *female archetypes* – original patterns that all women hold. They are:

- the dynamic young **Maiden**
- the gentle nurturing **Mother**
- the dynamic and mature **Enchantress**
- the wise and solitary old **Crone**

The four female archetypes of Maiden, Mother, Enchantress and Crone are the universal energies that are embodied by all women.

The energies and gifts of these four archetypes are expressed in the four phases of a woman's life, and in the four phases of her menstrual cycle. Just as we change in energy and awareness from a young girl to a fertile woman and from a mature woman to an old woman in our life cycle, we also change in energy and awareness from phase to phase during our menstrual cycle. Each phase of our life and each phase of our cycle has a different energy and a different focus, and all are equally a beautiful and amazing expression of being female.

These archetypes have two dynamic expressions of female energies – the Maiden and the Enchantress – and two receptive expressions – the Mother and the Crone. Recognising female energies in these terms not only **releases us from the limitations set by society's expectations** and labelling, it also frees us to explore our authentic femininity and to discover how we can express these energies into the world to create positive and harmonious change.

What it means to be feminine

To be 'feminine' is to express our Sacred Feminine nature, whatever our age, our level of fertility or our physical state. To be feminine is not just to be gentle and motherly, it is also to perceive ourselves as the young maiden, the dynamic warrior, the seeker of enlightenment, the empowered queen, the abundant giver, the weaver, the sexy enchantress, the beautiful witch, the wild woman, the poised priestess, the challenger, the walker of worlds, the grandmother of the world, the seer, and the ugly and powerful old witch.

Finding your Sacred Feminine

In many spiritual traditions there are definitive teachings on the Divine, but for women there is a unique and personal guide to the Sacred Feminine that is accessible to all. This guide connects us to Her presence and energies, offers help and support, and shows us how to create happiness and fulfilment. This guide to finding the Sacred Feminine lies within our body and our self-awareness.

Our body is our sacred text.
Our monthly cycle and our
life cycle are our prayers.

Our bodies are fundamentally the same as those of our female ancestors, and like them we can feel the presence of the Sacred Feminine within us and express Her in the world through Her many shapes and forms. Like our female ancestors we are 'The Moon on Earth' – expressions of the Sacred Feminine in all her forms. Like the moon we can only see a Cyclic Woman in her current phase – we cannot see the whole cycle or the whole woman. Like the moon we change phases, yet we remain the same. We are light and dark, outward and inward, moving and still, visible and hidden.

My book *Red Moon* explores in more depth the ancient wisdom about the menstrual cycle and the Sacred Feminine that lies in folklore and mythology, and its application to our lives.

Exercise: *What do I call you? Naming the Sacred Feminine*

Without definitive teachings on the Sacred Feminine, many women find it difficult to know what to call Her. Often the first thought is to Google 'Goddess names' and choose names from mythologies and traditions that are not from our own ethnic

---

background or from the land we live on. However, the Sacred Feminine does not belong to the past – She is living and vibrant in the women of today, and in the land around us and in the moon above us. Rather than use old names, we can use our intuition and creativity to inspire titles to call Her by.

Listen to Her voice in the different phases of your cycle, feel Her energies express themselves through you, and name Her after the energy, feelings, and images She brings you.

Watch the moon through her phases and the earth through her seasons and let the Sacred Feminine speak to you directly through your heart, your womb and your feelings.

If a title you create for Her fills you with love and your body relaxes when you think of the words, then this is the title She chooses to take in Her relationship with you in this phase of your cycle and of your life.

Dancing with the Sacred Feminine

We do not have to 'believe' in the Sacred Feminine, we simply experience Her presence in how we feel, in our changing energies and in the changes in nature around us. The Sacred Feminine is more than words or intellectual concepts – She lies in our nature, in who we are now, and in the expression of who we are. Every woman's experience of the Sacred Feminine will be different and unique, but that experience will be authentic for her and will create a real, interactive relationship that is based on mutual attention.

To consciously live with the Sacred Feminine is a dance where the music is always changing tempo and the Sacred Feminine guides us through the steps. She is our constant dance partner – sometimes leading, sometimes letting us lead, sometimes teaching us new steps and movements, but always guiding us as the music changes. When we partner Her we have the security to let go to the music, to be free and to let Her open us to new experiences of joy, wonder and magic.

Listen to your body. Listen to Her voice in your heart and in your womb. Relax and flow, and you will find Her in your life.

Why is the Sacred Feminine important for modern women?

Through Her nature, the Sacred Feminine shows us how to manage change, how to release the stress of being a woman in a masculine energy world, and how to value the changes of growing old, so that we stop fighting and embrace our true potential.

The Sacred Feminine as the key to managing change

The modern world is changing so quickly that we can often struggle to keep up with these changes. Changes that would have taken two or three generations are now taking two or three years. What our children are currently learning as essential life skills, life goals, values and approaches, will change several times before they have finished growing.

This increasingly rapid change and its ensuing lack of stability and security creates an on-going level of background stress in many women. When we are stressed we interact with the world from the most primitive aspect of our brain, and our life then revolves around survival, insecurity, self-focus and fighting rather than being focused on openness, love, joy, and being relaxed and generous. Any change, good or challenging, can become labelled as 'bad' because it upsets our sense of security.

But what if we were comfortable with change? What if we were able to embrace change in the world around us and within ourselves without it disrupting our inner sense of who we are, or threatening our self-love, self-belief and self-confidence? The Sacred Feminine gives us the key to managing change in our lives.

**The Sacred Feminine offers us a path
of graceful flow amidst life's changes,
guided by Her changing nature and the
experiences of our own cyclic nature.**

Women: The managers of change

Whether or not we are conscious of it, we women have an intimate wisdom and knowledge linked to change.

As women with a menstrual cycle
WE CHANGE every day.

Each day we journey a small step through our current cycle phase, leaving one phase behind and progressing towards the next. If we compare one day with the next it is difficult to see this change, but when we compare one week with the next (the approximate duration of the experiences of a menstrual cycle phase) we can see large differences in ourselves. *We live change* and we daily experience change as an integral and empowering part of being a woman.

The Sacred Feminine, expressed in the changing cycles of the moon and the seasons, shows us that we can be constantly changing and yet remain the same. She shows us the natural stages of change – the cycle of activity and rest – and She shows us that embracing change is not hard (after all it is our inherent nature). Rather, it is resisting change that is difficult and disruptive, and it is this that steals our energy.

When we recognise the Sacred Feminine in the world around us we see everything swaying to the eternal flow of Divine love and creation. When we recognise the Sacred Feminine in our cycles, She shows us how to live graciously with change – by accepting the cycle of action and rest and by seeing all changes as an opportunity to be creative in the world. She reveals that every experience shows us what we love and want and helps us to focus on that love to inspire us, to give us courage and to manifest our dreams. She carries us away from the daily roller-coaster ride of emotions and takes us deep within ourselves to a point of calm and strength at the centre of our cycle and at the centre of ourselves. This is the part of us that doesn't change – it is the part of us that expresses itself into the world through the different women we become in the different phases as we journey around the menstrual cycle.

The Secret to graceful change

By embracing our cyclic changes we gradually find it easier to also embrace changes in our external lives. We stop resisting our cyclic nature and start to acknowledge our changing thoughts and emotions. We accept ourselves more, which empowers us to accept the world and other people. It is in this self-acceptance that we find a place of calm strength and love that helps us to embrace all change with joy.

The Sacred Feminine as the key to the stress of being a woman in a man's world

As well as the stress of a fast-changing world, women also carry the additional stress of being **unable to live in harmony with their authentic nature**.

For most women between the ages of approximately ten years old to around fifty years old, our nature is cyclic. However, we are raised with the expectation of living and working and behaving like men. We are taught, unrealistically, to expect that the things that fulfil men and meet their needs will also make us happy and contented – and when we fail to be happy and fail to match these expectations we can feel guilt, anger and depression. The cry of 'Why do I feel like this?', 'Why do I act like this?' and 'Why can't I control myself' are heartfelt cries of pain from our deepest levels. The answer is that we lack understanding of who we are – Cyclic Women expressing the Sacred Feminine in all her cyclic beauty!

When we fight our nature in order to 'fit in' with expectations, when we repress or restrict ourselves or push ourselves to act in alien ways, we can create feelings of frustration and aggression towards ourselves – and these feelings spill out into the world around us. We are not 'bad' or 'wrong', we simply have **inappropriate expectations** of who we are and our deepest levels respond to this pressure by fighting for validation and for their needs to be met. As we journey through our cycle we naturally express different aspects of our authentic femininity, even if we are unaware of them, and it is our lack of understanding of these aspects of our self that increases our levels of frustration and stress and our heartfelt cry of 'Why am I like this?'

The Sacred Feminine validates our natural cyclic nature and shows us the benefits, strengths, and wisdom available in each of our cycle phases. As we acknowledge and welcome Her energies and presence in each phase we start to live our lives in new ways. We start to perform activities in specific phases because **they are easier to do**. We acknowledge the needs that lie in our phases – and when we do something to meet those needs we quieten the primal area of our brain that is programmed for 'lack and attack' and we live life from a more loving, generous and contented place. When we consciously carry out activities to express the energies within us, something amazing happens – we feel completeness, contentment, strength and balance. After the roller-coaster ride of emotions throughout the month, this can be a blessing in its own right!

Most of us live in a society where we cannot live a daily life completely in harmony with our cyclic nature, but we *can* do small things to meet our changing needs and to express the changing energies of the Sacred Feminine. Just by carrying out small activities in harmony with our phase, we start to relax the stress we carry and begin to create the feelings of inner strength and completeness inherent in our nature as women. Chapter 9 of this book provides a path of daily activities to use between the Worldwide Womb Blessings.

The Sacred Feminine gives us a role model of authentic femininity, She validates our female nature, and She helps us to embrace the changes this nature brings. By understanding Her nature within us we can live our lives in tune with our energies and changes, and dance a cyclic path in a linear world.

Exercise: Calling the Sacred Feminine home: Releasing stress through connection

So much of our modern-day stress is caused by a perception that we lack power or control. With modern technology and modern expectations we can have a continuously replenishing list of things we have to do – it's not surprising that we often feel out of control. Add to this our cyclic nature and our changing levels of energy and abilities, plus a society that doesn't support this amazing nature, and the feeling of being powerless can be overwhelming at times – especially in our pre-menstrual and menstrual phases.

When we open to the Sacred Feminine and actively try to live in harmony with Her nature, She brings us strength and centredness in our femininity, giving us the ability and power to make decisions and to take action. The following exercise opens us to the Sacred Feminine and gives Her a home in our womb and womb centre.

Sit comfortably with your palms turned upwards resting on your thighs or held level with your womb.

Close your eyes and bring your awareness to your womb and womb centre.

Take a deep breath and consciously relax the muscles of your lower belly.

Feel, imagine or intend that your womb centre opens out in all directions, enveloping your lower belly and hips.

In your mind say:

'I open my womb to the Sacred Feminine. Please come sit in my womb'.

Consciously relax this area of your body as you say the words.

Breathe gently as you repeat the words several times.

Relax in the experience and notice how you feel.

When you are ready to finish, imagine or intend that roots grow down from your womb centre into the earth.

Wiggle your fingers and toes, and open your eyes.

Have something to drink and to eat.

You may like to do this exercise once in each of your phases, or during the different phases of the moon. Notice how you feel and how the presence of the Sacred Feminine feels in your womb.

You may also like to use a beaded bracelet or necklace as meditation beads. Say the words once per bead.

The Sacred Feminine as the key to soulful menopause

When a culture validates the Sacred Feminine in all her aspects, women in their mature years also have their femininity valued. We have seen that our femininity is not just about fertility, but rather it is expressed in all aspects of a woman's life from birth to death. Modern society often places little worth on mature women and they can often live isolated and increasingly impoverished lives. Yet it is these women who stand at the doorway between the material world and spiritual world who have a deep wisdom and insight that is free from the social conditioning of the everyday modern world.

The prospect of worthlessness due to the lack of a fertile cycle and lack of youthful looks means that the change from the fertile Mother phase of life is so often wrapped in fear and loss.

It's no wonder that the change to being a post-menopause woman is stressful and that women fight hard to delay their entry into the last two archetypal phases of life – the Enchantress and the Crone. In our peri-menopausal and post-menopausal journey of dynamic, challenging changes we embody the Enchantress. As our energies slow and we are called by the soul to withdraw and focus on the spiritual side of life we embody the Crone.

The path to completeness

Women who connect with the Sacred Feminine can, however, see the value and strength in these later phases of life. They see that after the 'full' phase of the moon and the tide and after the abundance of summer comes a dynamic phase of wild energies and challenging change, and of deepening creativity and intuition. They also see that after the outgoing energies of the tide, the decreasing moon and the withdrawal of energies in the autumn comes a period of stillness, peace and oneness. In that period comes acceptance and deep spiritual awareness as the binding of the material world and the needs of the ego unravel. Life goes on at its hectic pace, but underneath it all they feel the pulse of the Universe and their place in something beyond imagination.

In the change from Cyclic Woman to a post-menopausal woman, we release the influence of the hormonal cycle and become more sensitive to the influence of the cycles of the moon and of the earth. Through these cycles we can enjoy a deep spiritual connection with the Sacred Feminine. If we fight our change from the hormonal cycle to the 'spiritual cycle', our life becomes stressful as we try to hold on to the out-worn aspects of our lives.

But when we see that our change from fertile woman to non-fertile woman is an aspect of the cycle of the Sacred Feminine, and we understand the new self-empowerment, spirituality and creativity this change in our life will bring us, we are more able to embrace any challenges and to welcome this new and exciting phase of our life. The Sacred Feminine shows peri-menopause and post-menopause women how to change, and the beauty within this change.

The post-menopause is not growing old, it is growing up.

The menopause change was never meant to be disruptive, but rather a harmonious blending of all aspects of our femininity into Oneness.

So how does the Sacred Feminine and Womb Blessing help us?

In this time of constant change and worldwide stress, connecting with the Sacred Feminine – by acknowledging Her in our bodies and feeling Her presence in our menstrual cycles, in the cycles of the earth and in the cycles of life – helps to bring us relief from the stress of modern life. We see that there is a natural female path that is different to society's expectation and it involves acknowledging:

- that we change
- that in the four phases of our cycle we are different women with different energies, needs and abilities
- that when we live in tune with this authentic femininity, we feel increased well-being, empowerment and love.

The Sacred Feminine shows us:

- that change is okay
- that we are strong and creative enough to flow with it
- that each of the stages of our lives takes us through a powerful change full of gifts.

The Womb Blessing attunement is a beautiful way for us to become more conscious of the Sacred Feminine within ourselves and within the world around us. Through this increasing awareness we can feel Her guidance in our lives as we walk a path towards self-empowerment, self-acceptance, self-love and becoming authentic in our femininity. Each Womb Blessing is a merging of our energies and consciousness with the Sacred Feminine so that we can awaken and embrace more of Her within us to ease our heartfelt pain of isolation and disconnection.

The Womb Blessing attunement also energises our womb centre, the source of our female strength and energies, awakening the aspects of the Sacred Feminine that have been buried or dormant. With each Womb Blessing we awaken more of our self, we discover more about who we are – our gifts and passions and our purpose in life. We are given the love and courage to live true to our awakening.

By journeying the yearly path of Worldwide Womb Blessing attunements, and awakening and living all the aspects of our femininity, the transition into post-menopause becomes more conscious, harmonious and graceful. The Womb Blessing helps women already post-menopausal to open to all aspects of their femininity, to enjoy this stage of life and to welcome and experience the beauty of oneness.

When we receive the Womb Blessing, the everyday stress that clouds our mind is blown away and for a while we rest bathed in the light of Sacred Feminine energy which illuminates our authentic nature. We come home to the Divine Mother and to ourselves as Her daughters. In Her light the barriers and blocks created by stress break down – healing our survival patterns, limitations and the fears that are so easily awoken by the pace of modern life. She fills us with a sense of centeredness and completeness, of empowerment and of being loved, so that we return to the world again aware of Her presence and we act from love rather than from feelings of isolation and heartache. As She awakens aspects of Her self within us, She helps us to recognise ourselves as reflections of Her being and all that we are is sacred in that reflection.

In our sacredness we know that we have the strength and creativity, wisdom and intuition to walk calmly on the waves of the storms.

Chapter 4: The Womb Blessing: A female energy awakening

One day First Woman decided to visit Earth Woman in her cave. When Earth Woman saw First Woman they hugged, and Earth Woman said 'The birds have been telling me about your beautiful bowl, may I see?'

First Woman opened the cloak which she had woven from many colours and showed her bowl to Earth Woman.

'Ah' said Earth Woman, 'now I see what it is for'.

She turned away and said 'I have a gift for you'.

When Earth Woman returned she held a stone pot full of paint, and with a brush she drew symbols on First Woman's belly.

'I give you the power of the air to create your heart-dreams' she said as she drew.

'I give you the power of fire to support your heart-dreams.'

As she drew a third symbol she said, 'I give you the power of water to bring magic to your dreams'.

And with the last symbol she said 'And I give you the power of earth to know your own power and your soul's dreams'.

Earth Woman stood back, satisfied.

'Hmm' she said, and she nodded.

Unwrapping the Womb Blessing

**The Womb Blessing attunement is
the sharing of
the love and light of the Sacred Feminine
by women for women to awaken.**

It has been a difficult process to describe the Womb Blessing - when we work with energy we work beyond the world of words and inhabit the world of feelings, intuition, inner wisdom and oneness. The Womb Blessing is opening like a flower, and we are still growing in our awareness of its beauty and purpose in the world. What started as an intention and a gift of energy has blossomed into an organisation that teaches women to give the attunement and, combined with the concepts and practical teachings in *Red Moon*, offers women not just an awakening but also an understanding of who they are and guidance on living the better way of life they feel they deserve.

The modern world likes definitions and certainties, but the feminine is creative, adaptive, flowing and changing. The joy and wonder of the Womb Blessing is to see it expanding in new directions and expressions, reflecting the needs of women and the creativity of all involved.

So what is the Womb Blessing?

The Blessing is the first energy attunement to the Sacred Feminine designed specifically for the unique energy structure of women and focused on the four female archetypes.

The attunement raises the vibration of the three main female energy centres and creates a deep and strong connection to the love and light energy of the Sacred Feminine. It awakens the full energies of the four female archetypes of authentic femininity, a process that begins with the attunement and continues for a month afterwards. The Blessing also connects the womb to the moon and the stars. It energises the womb centre and restores our female energies, and aligns our cyclic nature more fully with the cycles of the universal feminine. Finally, it grounds women strongly in the earth – connecting their womb to the Earth Mother – and calls their feminine soul back home to them.

The Womb Blessing attunement is given through a worldwide group womb-link, and also through Personal Womb Blessings offered by Moon Mothers.

The Womb Blessing attunement is a path of awakening and of receiving Sacred Feminine energy that is accessible to all women regardless of age, physical condition, life decisions, ethnicity or beliefs, and the Worldwide Womb Blessing community welcomes and includes the support of men. Women can take part in every Worldwide Womb Blessing and receive Personal Womb Blessings from Moon Mothers every month to create a quick and profound personal path of deepening healing and of personal and spiritual development.

The additional gifts of the Womb Blessing attunement:

As well as raising our vibration and awakening our authentic femininity, the Womb Blessing offers us additional gifts. These gifts are as individual as the women receiving the attunement, but many of the women taking part experience:

- **Physical healing:** The Blessing offers us deep healing, especially linked to the lower belly, the cycle, our womb and ovaries, and the physical changes associated with hormonal changes.
- **Emotional and mental healing:** The Blessing helps us to release the past and to clear old emotions, stresses and patterns, creating positive support for our body in its healing. It can also help us to love and accept our femininity more, to feel our purpose in life, and to create a new and better life for ourselves.
- **Cycle balance and harmony**: The Blessing can help us to balance our menstrual cycle and to bring harmony to the emotional and mental expression of its energies and phase archetypes.
- **Happiness and joy:** The Blessing helps us to release the guilt and restrictions placed on us, to bring a sense of self-worth and freedom, and to develop spiritual connection and guidance.
- **Peace and restoration**: The Blessing gives us a peaceful sanctuary from the stressful masculine world, bringing feminine restoration and inner reunion.
- **Replenished creative and sexual energies:** The Blessing heals the bond with the Earth Mother frequently broken by the hectic pace of modern life, so that our womb centre is naturally replenished in its creative and sexual energies.
- **Vitality:** The Blessing energises our womb energy centre – which is regularly depleted – bringing us feelings of being revitalised, centred and whole.
- **Sacredness of our body:** The Blessing connects us deeply to the light of the moon so that we grow in conscious awareness of the expression of the Sacred Feminine through our body, our cycles and the cycles of the moon and the Universe.

- **Empowerment:** The Blessing awakens our self-confidence and inner strength, empowering us to grow in our femininity and create better lives for ourselves.

The benefits of walking the Womb Blessing path

Receiving regular Womb Blessing attunements helps us to **stay connected** to the newly awakened aspects of our authentic nature in a world that constantly threatens to disconnect us. It helps us to continue to feel the **pleasure, happiness and well-being** that comes from living in harmony with our authentic nature.

The Womb Blessing and my books *Red Moon*, *The Optimized Woman*, and *Spiritual Messages for Women* complement and support each other. The Womb Blessing attunement is **the way in which we awaken** the hidden and dormant aspects of our four female archetypes, and my books show **how we can** live everyday life in small ways in harmony with our authentic nature so that we stay connected and grow in our expression of our truth, and in well-being.

The Worldwide Womb Blessing community of women

The Womb Blessing community grew from the desire of women to reach out to each other around the world and to share their love, their hope, their tears and their joy – as well as their photographs! Sharing our cyclic nature and having it validated prevents the isolation we can all experience from not being able to truly express our female energies in our everyday lives.

Following women's individual stories and growth brings wonder at how the Womb Blessing can change lives, and it inspires us to stay connected to the path of the Womb Blessing. Discovering how women are living and expressing their authentic nature, and how they are creating Worldwide Womb Blessing groups to spread the Womb Blessing, inspires us to do the same and to change not only our own lives but also the lives of other women.

The women in the community come from all ages and all backgrounds and have a wealth of passion, creativity, inspiration, knowledge, life experience and training. If we need help, the community is there for us. The Womb Blessing has always grown in an organic way based on the needs of women – we can be part of that growth and create the community we desire.

The Womb Blessing is a shared worldwide goal

The goal of the Womb Blessing is very simple: to help all women in the world to awaken to their authentic femininity through the Womb Blessing.

We support all women in their personal growth and awakening with love and understanding, and create healing and empowerment in women through sharing knowledge of their cyclic nature and of the four female archetypes. We aim to help women to create success, fulfilment and abundance through their personal expression and the application of their authentic femininity, and to create a legacy for future generations.

We also validate men in their own path of awakening to their authentic nature.

The Womb Blessing community acts as a bridge to lead women from present-world societal perceptions to the new world of authentic femininity. The women within the community are the guides – each guide has her own knowledge and understanding, and so there are as many paths to cross the bridge as there are women wishing to cross it.

Exercise: Try it!

Curious? Find out for yourself what the Womb Blessing feels like for you!

I would like to personally invite you to register for the next Worldwide Womb Blessing, and then please share your experiences with other women to inspire them to begin their own path of awakening and healing.

Sharing the invitation to register is a way for us all to reach out to the many women who feel lost in their lives, who don't know who they are or why they feel the way they do. It is a way for us to respond positively to the global cry from heart and womb and show that we understand, that we love and care, and that there is a way for all of us to feel whole, loved and strong and to change the world for the better.

Go to www.wombblessing.com and click on the *'register now'* link.

The Womb Blessing: A return to authentic femininity and soul-fullness

Our authentic femininity is the pattern of our original femininity that lies in our body, in our cells and in our DNA. It is the blueprint of our female nature that lies in the home of our soul – the womb energy centre.

The female soul expresses the Sacred Feminine through four energies and four levels of consciousness that flow from the womb centre and guide our heart, feelings and thought processes. These energies ebb and flow with the universal rhythm of the Cyclic Feminine. When we act and think in harmony with our authentic femininity and live more in tune with the flow of energy and consciousness, our heart opens in joy, well-being and happiness at being who we truly are.

**Loving pleasure is our guide back
to our authentic femininity
and our guide to living it in
the everyday world.**

The Womb Blessing attunement helps us to uncover our authentic femininity by clearing away the restrictions and layers of separation that have hidden our original form, allowing aspects of our female soul pattern to shine through to be consciously embraced and lived.

**Each Womb Blessing helps us to
regularly clean away
any new layers of separation
that our modern culture creates.**

The Womb Blessing also brings our everyday awareness back to the womb – the centre of our female soul. When our sense of who we are is centred in our womb and connected to the energy of the earth, our womb opens our heart centre and we live and think and act from love. Love releases our inner barriers and opens us, making us receptive. In our receptiveness we can open to the light and love of the Sacred Feminine and allow Her to fill us, easing the heartache and feelings of separation. We live life not with the head but with the **soul-womb**, feeling that we are able to share our true self with others.

A Worldwide Blessing: A 'soul group' awakening and healing

In each Worldwide Womb Blessing women are asked to register a chosen time from four options to receive the Blessing attunement. At each chosen time the women taking part are connected together through the womb-link by their soul energy. The Womb Blessing attunement sent to them at that time clears the blocks, restrictions and patterns that **they share in common** and awakens the same aspects of their female archetypal energies that they are **all** disconnected from. The aspects that are awakened are those that are the most important to the group.

The Worldwide Womb Blessing is like an orchestra where the energies of the individual women blend together to awaken and release a beautiful symphony – a specific pattern of female energies – into their being.

A Personal Womb Blessing: An individual awakening and healing

Miranda Gray Moon Mothers are trained to offer women an individual version of the Worldwide Womb Blessing attunement in one-to-one sessions. These Personal Womb Blessing attunements can be received once a month between Worldwide Womb Blessing events. The Personal Blessing focuses on clearing the patterns that the **individual most needs to heal at that time** and awakens the most important aspects of **her** female archetypal energies. It is like being a soloist, standing in the spotlight and creating your own unique song. The Personal Womb Blessing attunement can create very quick, deep healing, and result in immediate profound changes in a woman's life.

Both the Worldwide Womb Blessing and Personal Womb Blessings are deeply transformational and are specifically designed to work together to help women.

Exercise: Embracing your womb-soul as the beautiful centre of your being

The core of who we are as women lies in our womb centre and **it is our womb-soul and its energies that affects and drives our heart, our thoughts and our feelings**.

When we view the womb as the source of love that opens our heart and fills our mind, then we become grounded in our femininity and we feel the strength and power that is our birthright. We walk and love and think from the womb centre.

> Close your eyes and bring your awareness to your lower belly and your womb-soul centre.
>
> As you breathe in, relax this area and see or feel a beautiful, delicate peach-coloured rose lying in your womb centre. It has five petals that open in radiance and love in response to your attention.
>
> Notice how you feel.
>
> Notice how you start to relax.
>
> Notice any physical feelings.
>
> Notice how your heart feels as you focus on the peach rose within your womb centre.
>
> Enjoy the experience for as long as you wish.
>
> To end the exercise, take a deep breath, wiggle your fingers and toes and open your eyes.
>
> Take awareness of the rose, your womb and your womb-heart connection out into the world.

The attunement activations: Opening our head, heart and womb

The Womb Blessing attunement technique used both in the worldwide events and in Personal Blessings consists of a series of activations. These have been created by blending energy methods from different traditions, from observing the flows of energy through the female cycle, and from following the inspiration and guidance of the Sacred Feminine in the heart and womb and in the quiet moments of stillness in the hectic modern world.

Through breath-work and energy transmission, the three main female energy centres in the head, the heart and the womb receive the Womb Blessing vibration of Sacred Feminine love and light. Unlike in other energy systems such as the chakra system, these deep-level energy centres connect directly with each other. As the vibration of these energy centres changes, we change in consciousness and old patterns are released, returning us closer to our authentic nature. It is this powerful yet gentle change in vibration that creates transformation or awakening.

The Womb Blessing attunement begins with an **activation on the energy centre that lies deep within our brain** and which is the connection between our body and the light of the Sacred Feminine. It raises the vibration of the centre, opening it to the Universal Light, bringing the beauty and purity of the Universal Feminine through Her full moon aspect into our personal awareness.

The second activation is in the heart energy centre and anchors the softness and radiance of Universal Compassion and Love again through the Sacred Feminine in Her full moon aspect. As our heart fills with this energy we open and accept all, releasing the fear and guilt we hold about being female and about our lives, bringing feelings of gentle love, acceptance and healing.

The third activation is within the womb energy centre, raising its vibration with the light of the Sacred Feminine and opening it to the expression of Universal Love through moonlight. Raising the vibration releases the barriers and hardness within us, and allows us to open like a flower to joy. It brings our awareness back to the womb centre as the centre of our being. It releases the energies of our authentic femininity that have been blocked or disconnected, bringing harmony and balance to the flow of energies that is our cyclic female nature.

A year of Blessings: A path to wholeness

Each Womb Blessing opens us a little more to the rhythm of the Sacred Feminine as she flows through us, and each releases deeper restrictions and blocks, allowing more aspects of our female energies to be healed and freed into consciousness.

Each Womb Blessing re-energises our womb energy centre, which is regularly depleted by modern life, and strengthens its connection to the earth and to the moon to keep us grounded in our female energies and aligned with our cyclic nature.

Every year the five Worldwide Womb Blessings help us to grow into oneness with the ebb and flow of the Sacred Feminine. They help us to return to our centre in the changing seasons of our lives and our cycles, empowering us to let go of the things that no longer serve us and feel confident and fulfilled within the glow of love that comes from being whole in who we are.

The Womb Blessing is both a path and a sanctuary. Modern life does not support our authentic nature, and so everyday life can separate us once again from the energies the Womb Blessing has awakened within us. Regular Womb Blessing attunements maintain our connection with our authentic female energies, as well as awakening new aspects of ourselves. To receive the Blessing is to sit in a sanctuary of the moon, a quiet female haven in a masculinised world.

The Womb Blessings support us in living every day as 'authentic' women. By living authentically we stay heart-centred and empowered in the storms of life.

A creative approach: How you can use the Womb Blessing in your life

Each Womb Blessing can be used in different creative ways, depending on what we bring to it and how we wish to use it:

A Healing: Restoring our inner harmony and balance

We all need to heal.

We need to heal our body and create an accepting and loving relationship with it and with its changes. We need to heal and release the imbalance and disharmony created by ourselves, by relationships, and by the modern world. We also need to heal the female lineage that lies within our cells. We may not be consciously aware of the all the levels of healing the Sacred Feminine brings, but it continues working in our life after the attunement.

A Therapy: A uniquely female approach

Every time we receive the Womb Blessing attunement we reconnect to our female strength, creativity, and sexuality – whatever our age. From this feeling of reconnection and completeness we are more able to release the past, to let go of restrictive thoughts and learned behaviours, to dissolve our stress, and to return to the freedom of who we truly are. The result is that we start **responding** to situations in a different way, we make different decisions, and we walk **new paths of action**.

A Spiritual path: Dancing with the Sacred Feminine

Each Womb Blessing is a beautiful physical prayer that connects us more deeply with the Sacred Feminine, enfolding us in Her healing and love. We return to Her as Her daughter, remembering who we are and opening to deep levels of guidance, insight and peace. In each Blessing we trust and allow the Sacred Feminine to change our path in life and the way in which we walk it.

A Self-development path: A return to our authenticity

The Womb Blessing attunement changes our energy levels, altering the pattern of our thinking, consciousness and perception. The Blessing empowers us to think, live and take action in new and exciting ways in tune with our female energies.

An everyday rite of passage: Releasing the past to embrace the future

The presence of the Sacred Feminine in the Blessing reminds us that we are not alone, that She travels with us in life and that, however hard things are, 'all is well'. To receive the Blessing is to help us release more of the past, accept the present, and step into the future with joy, love, strength and self-belief.

A life-change rite of passage: Welcoming and celebrating the stages of your life

The Womb Blessing is a wonderful and loving way to acknowledge the transformations of life. It is a beautiful way to welcome a young girl into womanhood and an empowering means to acknowledge the magical transformation of menopause and motherhood. It is also a beautiful and empowering way to acknowledge and accept life when it is filled with loss and grief and challenging change.

What about men and the Womb Blessing?

In the modern western world, where we have come to expect equality, it is easy to confuse equality with being the same. Men do not have the same energy structure as women. They do not have the menstrual cycle energies and cyclic perceptive abilities that women have. They cannot embody the four female archetypes, or merge them within their consciousness in their mature years. They also do not have the energy structure to hold two soul energies within their bodies. Men have different archetypal energies – they connect to the divine in a different way, and their perception of the world and their creative expression is different to women because it is perceived through a different set of criteria within the masculine body.

Many women also ask: 'How do we get men to understand our female nature, and to change so that they accept this nature in relationships and at work?'

The role of women is not to change men, just as the role of men is not to change women. Instead, we are there to facilitate and validate the changes in the awareness and the expression of the energies of the opposite sex as they awaken into their own authentic state. As we women start to awaken and to accept and express our authentic femininity, our female energies will have an effect on our partners, families, work colleagues and society. Whether or not they are aware of the changes in us, they will respond to our energy change, or respond to the way we do things differently.

The wonderful gift we give to men is that as we become more authentically female we give them the space to become more authentically male.

The modern western world is masculine-dominant, but it is not authentically masculine. It is based on the primal fear patterns of status and survival, lack and attack. Men also need to be free to explore what it means to be authentically masculine – and this does not involve women telling them who they should be or how they should behave! Men need to work with their own body, their own hormones, their own perceptions and energy cycles. We cannot do this for them because *the sexes are different*.

The awakened woman can, however, offer men the gift of a broader experience of the feminine and of sex. By understanding his partner's changed energies and aligning with them, a man deepens his relationship with his partner, explores a wider experience of the feminine, and deepens his awareness of his masculinity in response to her authentic cyclic nature, or to the merged authentic female energies post-menopause. His partner's cycle becomes for him a physical journey of inner exploration as she experiences and expresses her cyclic nature, empowering him to connect with his own differing levels of being. His partner's merging into a Complete Woman post-menopause provides him with a unique experience, not just to interact with the wholeness of femininity in one woman at one time but to notice how his own masculinity changes and responds to the effect of the power, magic, beauty and wisdom of a Complete Woman.

Men supporting the Blessing

In the Womb Blessing we have a growing number of men who are supportive at many different levels of involvement. These men are called in their hearts to support the women in their lives in their healing and awakening – and it is beautiful to see so much love from the men who are involved. They are partners, family members and friends – men who want to see women awaken into their authentic nature and who want to discover and explore the wonderful journey of living with and loving these women in all of their expressions. For men who are spiritual in approach, the expression of the four archetypes through a woman provides them with an interactive personal relationship with the Sacred Feminine, who guides them through the female body to the realisation of their own sacred expression of the Sacred Masculine.

The Worldwide Womb Blessing is organic in its growth and development. The 'Meditation for Men' used in the Worldwide Womb Blessing today is a response to the number of requests made by both men and women for men to actively participate in the Blessing events while their partners, or groups, receive the Blessing energy.

Men are also able to receive a personal energy transfer of Sacred Feminine energy called *'The Gift'* from Advanced Moon Mothers trained in the technique. The structure of the energy activations and transfer was guided by men, and is available both for men and young boys to help them to connect to the Sacred Feminine and to feel Her validation of their authentic masculinity. It is also a gateway for men to begin to explore their own relationship with the Sacred Feminine, and is available to men at a distance on the Worldwide Womb Blessing days – see online for registration details.

Ancient wisdom for the modern world

In the past, many traditions and cultures perceived all things as being expressions of the Sacred Feminine, and all that is masculine as born from the feminine. Just as the seas and the stars are the body and expression of the Sacred Feminine's being and love, the masculine is also an expression of Her. For those of us who, through upbringing and life experience, are unable to open to, trust, or allow ourselves to be vulnerable to the masculine energies, it can be difficult to experience the sacred sexuality that can be expressed with a male partner. It can also be difficult for us to trust a divine masculinity if we have been brought up in a religion which is repressive of female nature. To know that the Sacred Masculine is an expression of the Sacred Feminine is perhaps the beginning of a healing.

Exercise: Meeting the Sacred Masculine

In mythology and folk tales the masculine appears as the son of the Mother in many forms – as the lover, the father/king, the guardian, and the wise one. Just as the female archetypes may be symbolised by animals in stories, so too are the Sacred Masculine energies.

In this meditation for women, based on the Guardian Meditation in *Red Moon*, we are going to use the image of a white stag, known in medieval stories as a 'white hart' – but you can also use the image of a white unicorn or a white stallion if they resonate better for you.

> Sit comfortably.
>
> Take a deep breath and bring your awareness into your body. Feel your weight on the cushion or chair. Feel how heavy you are.
>
> See, know or feel, that in front of you stands the most beautiful tree. Its trunk separates into two main branches which are full of deep green leaves, small white flowers and red jewel-like fruits. You know that this is the Womb Tree.
>
> The tree is surrounded by a shallow pool, and its roots grow down into the crystal clear water.

The tree stands in a beautiful summer landscape full of flowers and plants, birds and animals. The land is bathed in golden sunlight which is warm and caressing.

As you watch, the trunk of the Womb Tree alters, and a beautiful stag walks out of the tree to stand in front. His coat is pure white and radiant and his antlers are large, with nine points.

You feel His magic calling out to your heart, and you slowly step into the pool and walk towards His beauty.

Gently, in wonder, you lift your hand to stroke His nose, and you see that His eyes are dark and full of stars. His breath is sweet and full of the scent of summer.

You place your arms around His neck, feeling His love and the masculine strength in the warmth and muscles of His body. All the hurt and pain you have carried connected to the masculine releases in His love, and you relax completely into the embrace with Him. You feel totally accepted, totally loved, and safe and protected. Feel your tears carrying away your hurt and the hurt of your female lineage into the pool of water to be cleansed by the Earth Mother.

When you feel ready, stand back from the white stag and open your heart to Him. Open to accept the Sacred Masculine in the beauty of the moon and in the strength and life energy of the earth.

Take a moment to ask for guidance, help or protection, and thank Him for his love.

If you wish, you can continue the meditation by walking through the summer landscape with Him.

To finish, bring your awareness to your womb centre and your own Womb Tree lying in your lower belly. See, know or feel that the roots of your tree grow down deep within the earth.

Take a deep breath and open your eyes.

Chapter 5:
Receiving the Worldwide Womb Blessings

First Woman sat with her powers, wondering what to do. So she looked up at Moon Mother, and seeing that her face was increasing she went to the Hare clan. She stayed with them a week, and they taught her many skills.

When Moon Mother showed her full face, First Woman went to the Horse clan, and they taught her how to cook and make a home for herself and others.

As Moon Mother's face started to decline, First Woman went to the Owl clan and they taught her wild magic until finally Moon Mother told her it was time to leave.

First Woman then rested in the cave with the Bear clan, healing her past and watching the Universe within her bowl until Moon Mother emerged again in the sky and held out her hand for First Woman to follow her back into the light.

The Worldwide Womb Blessing days

The Worldwide Womb Blessings take place on five full moons each year, and to take part in each Blessing is to journey a path of female awakening while surrounded by a creative and loving family of like-minded women.

The call in the heart has always been to offer Womb Blessing attunements to as many women as possible worldwide. For this reason, the Womb Blessing is offered at four times during Womb Blessing Day to make it as accessible as possible to different time zones. Receiving the Worldwide Womb Blessing is free, and the administration and organisation is supported by kind donations and by wonderful volunteers, especially the numerous volunteer translators who provide the information and meditations in increasing numbers of languages.

The Worldwide Womb Blessing does not belong to any specific tradition or religion

The Sacred Feminine asks us to create a relationship with Her that is individual to our desires, our upbringing, experience, culture and interests, and that is based on our personal awareness of Her energies. We use the words, images and names for Her that resonate in our heart. Women from many different religions, and from none, have joined in and gained their own experience of authentic femininity through the Worldwide Womb Blessing attunements.

The days chosen for the Worldwide Womb Blessings are seasonal, reflecting the energies of the Earth Mother and her connection with the womb energy centre and the cyclic energies of women. Each Womb Blessing Day is held on or near the full moon, a day when the fullness of the light of the Sacred Feminine is radiant in the world. We women are daughters of both the Earth Mother and the Moon Mother – we hold both of their energies within our womb centre, and we flow in reflection of their cycles.

As the Womb Blessing started in the northern hemisphere, in Britain, the dates chosen are the full moons in the months of the main Celtic seasonal festivals:

> Full moon in February
> Full moon in May
> Full moon in August
> Full moon in October
> Full moon in December

The Celtic people lived close to the land and honoured the Sacred Feminine, and their festivals followed the seasons of the earth – Imbolc 2nd February the start of spring, Beltane 1st May the start of summer, Lammas 1st August the start of autumn, and Samhain 31st October the start of winter. The fifth Womb Blessing of the year takes part on the full moon nearest the winter solstice.

However, **the Womb Blessing is *not* culture specific**, and there many traditions that have different names and associations for the full moons in the Womb Blessing months: for example the May moon is also known as the 'Flower Moon' or the 'Dragon Moon' in some northern cultures.

So often in modern life we are disconnected from the rhythms of nature. By noticing and expressing the cycle of the land we live in we become more conscious of the personal connection we have to the cycles of the Universe through our female body.

For the southern hemisphere the seasonal calendar is reversed, and so the full moons in the Worldwide Womb Blessing months express the opposite aspects of the Sacred Feminine.

Exercise: Make your next Worldwide Womb Blessing a seasonal celebration

Not everyone lives in a temperate climate with four seasons. As each Womb Blessing approaches, notice the season around you, notice what the weather is like, how the plants are growing and how you feel.

- Give a name to the full moon at the time of each Blessing, either from your own cultural tradition or from your observations of nature.
- You may like to create a small altar for the Womb Blessing that expresses the energies of this season, the female images and animals you associate with it, and your feelings about it.
- **If you are running a Worldwide Womb Blessing group**, ask the women taking part to bring something for the centre of the room or space to express the energies of the season, and to bring foods that are traditional to this time or which are in season. Decorate the room in seasonal colours and plants and flowers.

Sharing the Sacred Feminine with other women

Many women are struggling to find spiritual fulfilment or purpose in their lives, but when we connect with the Sacred Feminine we can feel her voice in our hearts calling us to action to help other women. She also calls us to heal the land that we live on, and to reawaken it so that the Sacred Feminine energies envelop all that live there.

On Worldwide Womb Blessing day, the women taking part connect through their womb centres to create a network of Sacred Feminine energy around the world. After receiving the Blessing, women have the opportunity to use this womb-link network with the Sharing Meditation to send the love and light of the Sacred Feminine around the world. The event is not just one of giving, but because all the women taking part are connected we also receive at the same time as sending.

The joy of modern technology is that women in the Womb Blessing family may live in remote places and still feel that they are not alone in their awakening or in the exploration and expression of their female energies. The Sharing Meditation helps us to feel this connection and a sense of belonging to and helping a worldwide family.

Changing the world – one woman at a time

Every woman taking part in the Worldwide Womb Blessing has an active role in awakening the authentic female energies in the hearts, minds and wombs of women, and in changing the world. As the numbers of women taking part in the worldwide events grow, the energy shared increases, creating deeper healing, faster awakening, and a deepening of the conscious connection to the Sacred Feminine.

**We have seen that
as the number of women taking part
the Worldwide Womb Blessings has grown,
the higher the vibration of energy shared
the more energy shared,
and the deeper the effects**

Even if we can only take part in the Womb Blessing Meditation and Sharing Meditation for just a few minutes on Womb Blessing day, we not only receive the energy of the Sacred Feminine into our body and into our life, but we also make a personal impact on the lives of many women around the world.

We women have been restricted for so long that there is now a deep call within us to be the midwives to the birthing of a new world where masculine and feminine are individually authentic and live in a respectful, honouring and harmonised way.

Exercise: Register for the next Worldwide Womb Blessing

To register to take part in the next Worldwide Womb Blessing, go to www.wombblessing.com and click on the '*register now*' link.

You will need to supply your name, email address, country, and the language you would prefer to use. You will also be asked to choose one of the four times during the day when you wish to receive the Womb Blessing energy. Please note that the times given are times in the UK – you will need to find out what times these are in your own time zone.

The information you enter provides a focus for sending the attunement to you – and ensures that you will be reminded to register for the next Worldwide Womb Blessing day.

If you are taking part in a group, you will still need to register your own individual details, choosing the time that the group will be meeting to receive the Womb Blessing.

You will need to register separately for every Worldwide Womb Blessing in which you wish to take part.

Womb Blessing Day: How to take part

To receive the Worldwide Womb Blessing you simply need to:

1. Register for one of the four available times to receive the Womb Blessing attunement.
2. Download the instructions on what to do on the day. Documents are available on the website in a wide range of languages.
3. Download the additional Archetype Meditation – more information about these meditations is given in the next chapter.
4. Collect the items you need to take part – outlined below.
5. Sit comfortably at your chosen time, read the Womb Blessing Meditation, and relax to receive the Blessing. After 20 minutes you may do the Sharing Meditation and the additional meditations if you wish.

6.   Finish by eating and drinking something nice in celebration.

The Worldwide Womb Blessing can be received anywhere: in a bedroom, in an office, alone or with others, in a park, on the beach, in nature or in a public venue.

After the first Worldwide Womb Blessing, women started spontaneously to create regular groups to share the energy. So follow your heart and intuition to create your own group. Some groups are small, some are private, other groups are large public events or take place online or in virtual worlds. The Worldwide Womb Blessing is growing in a feminine way, an organic way, through the amazing passion, inspiration and creativity of the women called to take part.

Your Womb Blessing kit!

The Womb Blessing Meditation will take 20 minutes, and the Sharing Meditation can take an additional 10-15 minutes. These two meditations are the core of the Worldwide Womb Blessing and remain the same for every event. See Appendix for timing wheel.

To take part, you will need:

- **Two small 'womb bowls'.**

   These bowls need to be waterproof and fireproof. The bowls can be simple everyday kitchen utensils, such as cereal bowls, or they can be special bowls that you choose and keep just for this purpose.

   One bowl is filled with water to represent the Living Waters of the Womb. This water will absorb the energy of the Womb Blessing, and participants drink this water at the end of the meditation.

   A small tea light candle is placed in the other bowl and lit to represent the Light of the Sacred Feminine that we hold within our womb.

- **A copy of the Womb Blessing Meditation** and the Sharing Meditation, or download an audio version.
- **Something nice to eat and drink** for after the Blessing.
- **An upright chair**, or cushions on the floor.
- **A shawl to wear.** A shawl helps to create a sacred space around you and helps you to focus your awareness inwards.

Before your Worldwide Womb Blessing

- Find or buy two bowls to use as womb bowls. If you have time, choose something that reflects your feelings about your womb, your femininity, the Blessing and the Sacred Feminine. Look for colours, patterns and bowl shapes that express your feelings.
- Buy or make a special shawl to wear for the Womb Blessing. You may like to choose a colour that reflects your feelings about the Sacred Feminine, or one that expresses your current menstrual cycle phase.
- Make a playlist of your favourite music to have as background music during the meditations.
- Choose a perfume or essential oil to wear which expresses your cycle phase or the season.
- Choose items to decorate a room or an altar to create a sacred space for taking part.
- Print out the meditations to use, or download the audio.
- Make some moon-themed food to eat in celebration afterwards.
- You may like to do the 'Stirring the Cauldron' meditation featured in chapter 2 a few days before the Blessing to help you connect to your womb in preparation.

During the Blessing

To start:

- Sit comfortably with your womb bowls in front of you.
- Place some drinking water in the womb bowl on your left. Then, if it is safe to do so, light the tea light and place it in the womb bowl on your right.
- Place your shawl around you.
- Have the text for the meditations ready.

At your registered chosen time:

1. Slowly read the **Womb Blessing Meditation,** giving yourself time to visualise or feel each stage.
2. Sit relaxed and be open to receive the Blessing until 20 minutes after your chosen time. So if your chosen time is 06.00, you will receive until 06.20.

3. Open your eyes and read the Moon Ray meditation and then the **Sharing Meditation** – taking time to send the energy at each stage.
4. At the end of the Sharing Meditation, wiggle your fingers and toes and take a deep breath. Slowly drink the water from your womb bowl, connecting with the energy it has absorbed.
5. Move very gently and eat and drink your special food as a celebration of the physical presence of the Sacred Feminine.
6. The Womb Blessing attunement can create a little detox, so make sure that you drink more water during Womb Blessing day and on the day after.

If you wish to do the additional Archetype Meditation after the Sharing Meditation, follow the instructions given in the appropriate text available to download after registration.

Womb Blessing days are very special. We have opened to the presence of the Sacred Feminine and connected with thousands of women around the world to awaken Her energies once again in the world and in the hearts and minds of all. For some of us the experience will be physical, for others visual or emotional, and for yet others it can be one of peace and deep guidance.

It is important that we are gentle with ourselves during Womb Blessing Day – we have entered a sacred space and for a while we have sat in the presence of the Sacred Feminine, and the transition back into the noise and activity of everyday life can feel a little bit of a shock.

Exercise: Run your own Worldwide Womb Blessing group!

Anyone can run a Worldwide Womb Blessing group – and the more creative and individual they are the better!

When we receive the Worldwide Womb Blessing in a group we can have a deeper experience of the energies and feel safe and supported walking our Womb Blessing path.

Whether there are just two of you in a group or 100, the energy is enhanced.

To be in a group of women resonates within our wombs and female energies, and it is time that we brought this experience back into the modern masculine world. So…

Start small – especially if you have not run a women's group before.

Ask women to bring a friend.

Tell women that the Womb Blessing is a journey of awakening and healing and encourage them to take part in all five Blessings.

Remind women when the next Worldwide Womb Blessing is going to be.

Tell women which chosen time they have to register for your group, and where they should register online.

Make a checklist.

Trust your heart and have courage.

The Worldwide Womb Blessing is free, but you may wish to charge a small fee to pay for venue hire, printing materials or buying food, water, flowers and any other items needed to run the event.

Common questions about the Worldwide Womb Blessing

What does the Womb Blessing feel like?

We are all individual in the way we experience our body, cycles and energy, and in our relationship with the Sacred Feminine. Some of us are very body-aware, and we may feel physical sensations. For those of us who are feeling-aware, we may experience feelings of love, joy, peace, expansiveness, grounding, or deep emotions as we release old patterns. If we are very visual, we may 'see' colours, scenes and images.

Every Blessing can be a different experience as our energies are changing each time and we become more open and more aware at all levels of our female energies.

**The Womb Blessing energy is constant,
it does not change with the season, the
moon phase, or our menstrual phase,
but *our experience* of the Womb Blessing
can change with these cycles.**

The Blessing asks us to open to the Sacred Feminine, and in particular to open our wombs. For some of us this may be challenging. Trauma – physical, emotional or mental – can be held in our lower belly area, and so we may resist relaxing and opening this area of our body. As we receive more Womb Blessings we find that we are able to relax and open more easily, and we start to be more comfortable with this area of our body – and we are then able to experience the Blessing more fully.

Do I need to do anything special?

To receive the Blessing you simply need to read the Womb Blessing meditation at your registered chosen time and to relax to receive the awakening. You do not need to do any special breathing techniques or mudra hand positions or body positions. You do not need to visualise in minute detail the meditation, or use your will and your focus to force things to happen. Our intention and relaxation during the meditation is enough to receive the energy.

Will I change? Will I heal?

In the moment that we receive the Blessing energy we change, whether we are aware of it or not. The changes that the Womb Blessing attunement brings can be dramatic, or they may be gradual over many months or years. The Blessing can shape who we are, how we feel, what we do and how we live, and can inspire us to take this awareness and allow it to grow in our lives.

We cannot predict how each Womb Blessing will affect us and we cannot direct it to heal or change anything specific. It may be that there is something more important to heal first that we are unaware of. The Blessing energy is Sacred Feminine Love, and so all changes are created by Her and are for our highest good and in accordance with Divine Love.

Can I change the words of the meditations?

It is important to use the words of the meditations as they are written, whether you are reading them on your own or in a group. The Womb Blessing Meditation is an energy process, specific to the female energy structure, and designed to prepare a woman to receive the Womb Blessing attunement. If the words are changed, you will have a nice meditation – but you will not receive the transformational Womb Blessing attunement.

Also, as more and more women around the globe use the same words, the meditation is growing in strength, making it quicker and easier for everyone taking part – whether they are beginners or experienced meditators – to connect deeply to the Womb Blessing vibration of Sacred Feminine energy.

Who can take part?

The Womb Blessing, either in the worldwide events or given in person by a Moon Mother, is available to all women, whatever their age.

Young girls

Young girls can take part in the meditations, but to register and receive the Womb Blessing energy they need to have had their first menstrual bleed.

Taking part in her first Worldwide Womb Blessing is a wonderful way for a young girl to celebrate her passage into womanhood.

Women with hysterectomies

Women without a womb can take part in the Blessing because they still have a womb energy centre and still embody the four female archetypes.

Post-menopause women

For women in peri-menopause, and for post-menopausal women, the Womb Blessing is a powerful way to connect with the energies and aspects of all the archetypes, especially those that have been lost or unfulfilled in their lives, and to gently and elegantly walk into the Complete Woman stage of life.

Pregnant women

Pregnant women can receive the Worldwide Womb Blessing attunement. The energy is transferred in a way that allows the baby to choose whether or not they wish to receive the energy. For the guidelines on receiving the Personal Womb Blessing, please ask your Moon Mother.

Sexual identification

Any person who resonates with the Womb Blessing Meditation, whatever their sexual orientation or identity, can access the Womb Blessing attunement. This is because the meditation is the method by which you prepare to unwrap the gift of the Womb Blessing attunement.

> If you feel a change in energy or awareness within yourself when you do the Womb Blessing meditation, it indicates that you are able to connect to the Womb Blessing energetically and you may like to join the next Worldwide Womb Blessing. Then listen to your heart to tell you whether to receive a Personal Womb Blessing.

> If you don't feel a change in energy or awareness when doing the Womb Blessing Meditation, it simply means that at this moment in time the Womb Blessing is not your path for connecting to the Sacred Feminine, and that there is a different path for you.

The modern world has a very limited view of femininity and masculinity. It is up to each of us to discover what these concepts mean to us, and to be free and unrestricted in expressing ourselves.

All the meditations and activities in Chapter 9 that feature the female archetypes can also be used by anyone without a womb or a menstrual cycle by following the path of the lunar or seasonal cycles instead.

Men

Some Worldwide Womb Blessing groups include men – and some couples like to do the Womb Blessing together. Most men cannot receive the Womb Blessing attunement because of their energy structure, however they can take part in a number of meditations for men, and they can register to receive The Gift on Womb Blessing day.

What if I miss my chosen time to receive?

Life is busy, so don't worry – you can still receive the attunement at any time **after** your chosen time by doing the Womb Blessing Meditation and sitting relaxed for 20 minutes. However, the experience won't be as powerful or as deep as when you take part at the same time as all the other women worldwide.

After the Womb Blessing

The Womb Blessing attunement that you receive on Blessing Day starts a process of 'birthing' into a new woman. The Womb Blessing energy begins to work through each of the four female archetypes – in alignment with the menstrual cycle phase or the lunar phase – throughout the following month.

As we birth, we clear away the old physical, emotional and mental patterns we no longer need for each specific archetype. It is therefore important for us to be more gentle with ourselves over the month, and checking the details in Chapter 8 of this book can help us to understand the type of archetype healing and awakening being made. Feeling more emotionally sensitive, a few aches and pains, or experiencing old fears or thought patterns, are all good signs that we are clearing and birthing into a more authentic femininity. Occasionally we may need a little extra help with our birthing or with our cyclic energies, and Moon Mothers offer the loving and embracing *Womb Healing – Female Energy Balancing*, for whenever we feel this need.

It can also be very helpful and rewarding to follow the flow of energy throughout the month after the Womb Blessing by making a note each day of your cycle phase and of your emotional, mental, physical and spiritual experiences. In a busy world there may not be much time to write notes, and the *Moon Dial* technique offered in *Red Moon* is a quick way to observe and enjoy the awakening of the new energies. It can also be useful to keep track of your phases during the month, as after the attunement some women can experience a slight change in the orientation of their cycle against the lunar cycle, making menstruation for this month occur a little later or earlier.

After the Blessing attunement we need to start to live in little ways in alignment with our cycle phases (or lunar phases if we do not have a cycle) to ground our new female energies into everyday life. **If we do not start to live in harmony with our female archetypes and their energies, we simply become separated once again from the wonderful feelings of wholeness, empowerment, and self-love that they bring.** 'The Womb Blessing Path' outlined in Chapter 9 introduces you to living in harmony with your inner female archetypes, and you can also explore further suggestions of cycle activities for work and goal-achievement in *The Optimized Woman*, and for creative and spiritual expression in *Red Moon*.

Exercise: Supporting your awakening

Blessing Day and the day after:

- Be gentle with yourself. If possible, have a quiet day where you can rest, meditate or walk in nature. This will help you to continue to be aware of the beautiful Sacred Feminine energy moving through you. Have a Sanctuary Day, where you nurture the femininity within yourself.
- Make sure you drink lots of water to support any detox effect of the energy.
- Make sure you eat regularly. When we experience big vibrational changes, our body uses its energy to integrate these changes, and we can feel tired immediately afterwards, a few hours afterwards, or the day after. It is important to eat healthily and to rest, to give your body the opportunity to renew its energies.
- **If you are pre-menstrual or menstrual when receiving the Blessing** it is important that you eat, drink and sleep more. The pre-menstrual phase is a natural phase of declining physical energy, and so it is important that you support your body by doing less and resting more. This is also true for the menstrual phase, which is your natural phase for restoring your energies and resting.
- Start a journal, or create a Moon Dial.

During the first week after Blessing Day:

- Be gentle with the people around you. Your vibration is changing, and although family and friends may not be conscious of it they will be sensing that you are changing. Just as it will take you a little time to get used to your new energy, they will need time too – and may need a little extra reassurance from you.
- Give yourself five minutes of self-healing every day using the simple technique given in the Womb Blessing document. This will support you through any clearing of old patterns and will help you to feel centred, empowered and loved in everyday life.
- If you need someone to journey with you, you can join one of the many Womb Blessing groups online, or contact an Advanced Moon Mother for mentoring.
- If you want some extra energy support, contact a Moon Mother for a *Womb Healing – Female Energy Balancing.*

During the second week:

- Continue to journal and give yourself daily healing.
- Do the **'Womb Blessing Meditation'** two or three times during the week for 10-15 minutes. You will be creating a sanctuary of Sacred Feminine energies where you can let go of stress and recharge your female batteries.

During the third week:

- Make it a priority in your life to live in little ways in tune with your cycle of energies.
- Continue to give yourself healing and to create your Female Sanctuary through the Womb Blessing meditation.
- You may like to draw a message for your phase from my book *Spiritual Messages for Women* to give you support.

During the fourth week:

- Continue to give yourself healing and to create a Female Sanctuary for yourself.
- Journey deeper and make receiving the Womb Blessing part of your path of personal and spiritual growth into love. Contact a Moon Mother to receive a Personal Womb Blessing attunement.

- If you want to work more deeply with your cyclic nature and personal awakening, contact an Advanced Moon Mother for Womb Blessing Mentoring.
- Finally, if your heart calls you to help women to heal and awaken through giving the Womb Blessing attunement and sharing the Worldwide Womb Blessing, become a Moon Mother!

Exercise: Self-healing meditation

You can do this meditation every day for 5-10 minutes or longer, to help support your awakening and healing.

Sit or lie comfortably with your hands over your womb.

Imagine a large full moon above you, filling your womb with beautiful silvery white light.

Allow the energy to flow through you – you may feel it in your hands and womb as a physical sensation. Not everyone senses the energy as it flows – every individual has their own unique experience of the energy – but it will be flowing into you.

Relax and enjoy!

To end, take a deep breath, wiggle your fingers and toes, open your eyes and smile. Then thank the Sacred Feminine for the healing.

Chapter 6:
The Womb Blessing meditations: Understanding and sharing our female spirituality

First Woman was busy. Using the powers of her bowl, she had created many things. Her home was filled with her loom and spinning wheel, baskets were stacked by the door with her pots, fresh bread baked in her oven outside, and she sat and shelled peas in her garden. All was well.

But then the Fox came.

Fox had watched First Woman create beauty and wonder, and he was jealous and wanted her power for himself.

'Hello First Woman,' he said, bowing low, 'how wonderful is your beauty, and how amazing your powers!'

'But,' he said slyly, 'I have noticed that you never seem to have each power for very long. They seem to go away, leaving you without them. How can you live like that?'

First Woman smiled.

'I know that they will always come back, so I just wait until they do.'

'But how do you really know?' asked Fox. 'What if they don't come back? You'll have nothing. Surely it is better to be the same all the time, then you can feel secure!'

First Woman hesitated, doubt and worry starting to form in her mind. Fox saw that he was winning.

'Look how difficult and negative your powers make your life. It's frightening not having control of yourself, not knowing how you will be or what you can do. You are better without them.'

First Woman looked at the objects on her power belt.

'How would I get rid of them?' she asked.

'Oh that's easy' said Fox. 'I can help you. Just give them to me. Without your powers constantly interrupting you, you can focus on being the same all the time. And your bowl will lose its power over you.'

He smiled. 'The fear of losing control will be enough to stop your powers coming back.'

First Woman felt her inner fear awaken. She felt the fear of not having control over her body or herself, and guilt at not being good at everything all the time, not reacting in the same way all the time, or feeling the same all the time.

'The bowl is not a good source of power' she declared. 'It's stopping me from doing what I want to be and do!'

'Yes' agreed Fox, holding out his paw.

The Womb Blessing Meditation: A profound experience of the female energy structure

The Womb Blessing Meditation below is the main meditation that, since the first Worldwide Womb Blessing day, has been shared by all the women around the world who have taken part.

> Close your eyes and bring your awareness into your body.
>
> Feel your weight on the cushion, the weight of your arms in your lap. Take a deep breath and feel centred within.
>
> Bring your awareness to your womb; see, know, feel or imagine that your womb is like a tree with two main branches, and beautiful leaves and red jewel-like fruits on the end.
>
> Feel or imagine that the roots of the tree grow down deep within the darkness of the earth, connecting you and anchoring you, allowing you to receive golden energy into your womb.
>
> Feel grounded and balanced.
>
> *(Pause)*

Now allow the image of your Womb Tree to grow until the tree's branches separate at the level of your heart.

As you connect with this image, see or feel your heart centre open and energy flow down your arms into your hands and fingers.

(Pause)

Feel the connection of love between the earth, your womb and your heart.

(Pause)

Still in awareness of your heart, look up and see or feel that the tree's branches continue to reach upwards to cradle a full moon above your head. The beauty of the full moon bathes you in a pure silver-white light that washes through your aura and over your skin.

(Pause)

Open to receive the light of the moon. Allow it to enter through your crown and fill your brain with light.

Relax further, and receive this light into your heart.

Relax even further, open your womb and allow this energy into your womb in blessing.

The Womb Blessing Meditation: The origin of the Womb Tree

The Womb Blessing Meditation is based on the ancient image of the **Moon Tree** found in early cultures, and its association with female energies. We first meet the Womb Tree as a personal image of the sacred Moon Tree in the chapter entitled *'The Awakening'* in my book *Red Moon*.

'The Awakening' is the story of a young girl named Eve and the dream that she has on the night of her first menstruation. Eve's story resonates with the female archetypes and symbols within us, helping them to awaken in our conscious mind to create a language of words and images that we can use to understand our cyclic nature. The story is an introduction to our cyclic nature.

In *'The Awakening'*, the Moon Lady takes Eve on a journey to meet the different women and goddesses who represent the energies of the phases of the menstrual cycle.

This is how Eve first meets her Womb Tree:

> "The Moon Lady brought them out into a clearing, at the centre of which stood a beautiful tree with a silvery-pink trunk. The trunk divided into two outstretched branches containing a bounty of red fruits and the full moon seemed to sit in the upper branches, its light reflecting in the pool of dark blue water surrounding the small island on which the tree grew. Twisting roots hung from the soil into the waters of the pool.
>
> 'This is your Womb Tree,' said the Moon Lady, and she touched Eve's belly just below her navel. In answer to her touch, Eve felt a warmth grow around the presence of her womb lying within her body. In front of them, the Womb Tree responded, glowing with energy."

Exercise: Meeting your Womb Tree

This meditation, based on one from my book *Red Moon*, introduces you to your own Womb Tree, enabling you to create an interactive and positive relationship with your womb and your cycle.

Sit comfortably, take a deep breath and relax.

See, know or feel that you are standing surrounded by a silvery mist.

As the mist gradually parts, you walk into a warm, moonlit glade.

In the centre of the glade you see a large tree on a mound rising from the middle of a circular pool. The trunk is silvery-pink and splits into two branches, each one ending in clusters of leaves and shining red fruit. Above the tree, a full moon floods the scene with silver light.

This is your Womb Tree.

How does your Womb Tree feel to you? Is it well, does it feel loved, does it respond eagerly to your attention?

(Pause)

The tree seems to shimmer with energy and you feel a deep resonance, both in your mind and in your womb.

(Pause)

You walk to the edge of the pool. The water is dark, and you can see the roots of your Womb Tree disappearing into its depths.

Looking into the water, you see your own reflection with the moon dancing above you, and you open to the mysteries of the universe lying within the water.

Intuitively you feel the universal link between women and the moon, the womb and the moon's cycle, and the magical link between your womb and your mind, and your mind and your womb.

Again you feel a deep resonance in your mind and in your womb.

Stay for a while, feeling your connection to your Womb Tree.

(Pause)

When you are ready to leave, allow the warm mists to once more cover the scene and gradually become aware of your body.

Take a deep breath, open your eyes and acknowledge your Womb Tree lying in your lower belly.

Over the years the image of the Womb Tree and the 'Magical Womb' meditation given in Chapter 2 evolved into a number of different meditations, providing the energy work, inspiration and experience needed to create the current Womb Blessing Meditation. The Womb Blessing Meditation is one of love, reconnection, realisation and joy – and a way for us individually to open our uniquely female energy structure to the Sacred Feminine and say **'I am ready to receive your energy and presence into my life'.**

The Womb Blessing Meditation can be used at any time as a personal meditation, but it has a very significant role in the Womb Blessing: **it is the method by which women open to the Sacred Feminine to receive the attunement.** The Womb Blessing is like a parcel, and the meditation is the way in which we receive the parcel and unwrap it so that we can accept transformation into our body and life.

A Womb Blessing attunement always consists of two main parts:

1. **The Womb Blessing Meditation** which connects us to the Sacred Feminine through the energy structure of our body, opening us to receive the attunement.
2. **The transfer of a specific vibration of Sacred Feminine love and light energy**, through the Womb Blessing attunement technique.

In all Womb Blessing attunements, whether a worldwide attunement or a personal attunement from a Moon Mother, the words of the meditation are read **exactly as they have been written**. No matter what language a woman speaks, all women around the world use the same Womb Blessing Meditation to connect to the Sacred Feminine and to open to receive Her gift of the Womb Blessing energy. The more women that use the meditation, the more the vibration of the words and energy expands in the world.

Grounded in the earth: The roots of the Womb Tree

The Womb Blessing Meditation is more than a simple visualisation – beneath it lies a profound spiritual experience of the female energy structure.

Most modern spiritual paths, religions or philosophies are strongly influenced by male thought and experience. They tend to be 'transcendental' in nature, offering a way to escape the material world for the spiritual world, the Light, or a higher non-materialistic level of being. We are taught methods to achieve this which often arise from the experiences of men but which are generalised as a path for both men and women.

However, the transcendental path is not the natural spiritual approach for many women. Our essential spirituality is one of being of the earth and of being a Light-Bearer. For us the physical world is intuitively the body of the Divine, whatever form She takes, and so it is intrinsically sacred. Our natural spiritual path is to embrace the Divine in the physical world around us and in our bodies, and to open to Her spirit or Light and bring it into the world. Our path is not one of rejecting the world or escaping it – it is one of loving and accepting the world and of embracing it.

Our spiritual path is not to escape but to embrace the world.

To be a Light-bearer – a conscious vessel for the energies of the Sacred Feminine – we need to connect deeply with the Sacred Feminine in her physical expression and with her energies of life. In the Womb Tree Meditation we do this by imagining or feeling that we grow 'roots' down from our womb and womb energy centre, deep into the earth. Our roots grow naturally from our womb out between our thighs and down our legs into the earth.

Take a moment and do this now:

Close your eyes and take a deep breath.

Bring your awareness to your womb centre. See, know, feel or imagine that your womb is like a tree with two main branches, with beautiful leaves and red jewel-like fruits on the end.

Feel or imagine that the roots of the tree grow down deep within the darkness of the earth, connecting you and anchoring you, allowing you to receive golden energy into your womb.

Relax and hold this image or intention in your mind.

Notice how you feel.

When we consciously grow our Womb Tree roots down to connect with the Earth Mother, something wonderful happens. The Earth Mother responds to our attention, and her energy naturally flows up through the Womb Tree roots into our womb centre. It doesn't matter whether or not we are aware of this flow of energy, it happens automatically. This energy is the energy of strength and life, sensuality and connectedness to the manifest world – it is wholeness and completeness. It energises our womb centre, calling our female soul back to us.

How do you feel now as you sit relaxed with your womb centre connected to the womb of the Earth Mother?

Something else happens when we connect our womb centre to the Earth Mother. As her energy flows into our womb and fills it, the energy naturally flows upwards to open and fill the energy centre at our heart. It then flows from the heart centre into our breasts and down our arms and into our hands. This flow of energy happens whether we are aware of it or not.

In the Womb Blessing Meditation we simply follow this flow of energy by imagining or intending that our Womb Tree grows upwards to the level of our heart.

Now allow the image of your Womb Tree to grow until the tree branches separate at the level of your heart.

As you connect with this image, see or feel your heart centre open and energy flow down your arms into your hands and fingers.

How does this feel?

We can use this first half of the meditation in the morning as a wonderful way to ground ourselves in our female energies, to feel strong and centred, and to step out into the world empowered and loving. When the womb centre is connected to the earth and energised, we can recognise that our lives and our self are a continuous cycle of changing seasons and we can surrender to this change with grace and trust.

Holding the Moon: The branches of the Womb Tree

In the second half of the meditation we stay at the level of our heart. We could journey upwards to the moon – but travelling upwards towards the Light is the masculine transcendental path. Instead we open to the moonlight and allow it to flow downwards into us, and through us out into the world. This is the female path of imminence, the path of being in the presence of the Divine in the moment and in the world. **It is the path of being the 'Moon on Earth'.**

Still in awareness of your heart, look up and see or feel that the tree's branches continue to reach upwards to cradle a full moon above your head. The beauty of the full moon bathes you in a pure silver-white light that washes through your aura and over your skin.

(Pause)

Open to receive the light of the moon. Allow it to enter through your crown and fill your brain with light.

Relax further, and receive this light into your heart.

Relax even further, open your womb and allow this energy into your womb in blessing.

If you can't visualize easily, or don't feel anything physically, it doesn't mean that the energy isn't flowing – the Sacred Feminine will respond to your intention and you may experience the energy flowing in other ways, such as in feelings and emotions, or in peace, love and calm.

In the Womb Tree Meditation we connect to the Earth Mother to become empowered women who are strong in our bodies, in our femininity, in our sacredness and in the sense of who we are. Once we are centred in our female energies we are able to open ourselves without fear or restriction to allow the presence of the Sacred Feminine to fill us. It is wonderful to do the complete meditation in the evening.

To finish the meditation, draw your Womb Tree back down into your lower belly, and be aware of its roots in the earth.

The Sharing Meditation: Sharing the love and light of the Sacred Feminine

When our heart opens we naturally want to share.

In the Worldwide Womb Blessing there is a second meditation called the **Sharing Meditation,** designed for women to do after they have received the Womb Blessing attunement. In the Worldwide Womb Blessing we are all connected through a network of energy that links all the women taking part, through their wombs, hearts and consciousness. We become a powerful network of female energy and sacredness. It can be a beautiful experience to feel the connection of so many other women sending us the love and light of the Sacred Feminine – even if we are physically alone in our awakening, we know that energetically and emotionally we are part of a wonderful female family worldwide.

The Sharing Meditation also focuses on sending the Sacred Feminine energy to the world, and to grounding the energy in the land in which we live. When the land awakens to the vibration of the Sacred Feminine, all that walk on the land will be enfolded in Her loving arms, and as love becomes part of their vibration so their lives will change.

Like the Womb Blessing Meditation, the Sharing Meditation below can be used daily, and it offers us a way to help the healing and awakening of women by sharing the love and beautiful presence of the Sacred Feminine. However, when the Sharing Meditation is used within the Worldwide Womb Blessing it becomes more powerful because of the connection of thousands of women taking part at the same time.

> Be aware of the moon above your head, and allow its energy to bathe you with light. Feel the light fill your head and your heart and flow down your arms to your hands.

(Pause)

Allow the energy to flow from heart and hands into the World.

Feel it flow out into other lands, changing the vibration to one of the Sacred Feminine.

Feel it healing, loving, soothing and nurturing the whole world.

(Pause)

Feel the presence of all the other women around the world who are connecting with this energy at this time. Send it to them – and receive it from them – in love, sharing and communion.

(Pause)

Now allow the energy from the moon above to flow from head to heart to womb and down into your Land.

Let the energy awaken and heal the sacredness of the Land and the Sacred Feminine within the Land.

(Pause)

Bring your awareness back into your body.

Feel your weight on the chair or the cushion, and gently move your fingers and toes. Take a deep breath and open your eyes.

The Moon Mother Full Moon Meditation

The Worldwide Womb Blessing can be like a Tibetan Singing Bowl, where we hit the bowl to create a note and then gently stroke the rim of the bowl to continue the singing of that note. Each Worldwide Womb Blessing event is like striking the bowl and creating a particular vibration of the Sacred Feminine in the world (the Womb Blessing energy). The **Moon Mother Full Moon Meditation** occurs on the full moons *between* the worldwide events to continue the note of the Sacred Feminine singing in the world.

As part of their service to women, Moon Mothers send the Womb Blessing vibration of the Sacred Feminine energy to all women in the world over the three days of the full moon. They send energy to all aspects of femininity, to the land, and to all women who suffer. This is not a transformational attunement, but a heartfelt sharing of healing and love.

Although the sending of the energy is a Moon Mother-only event, any woman can use the Womb Blessing Meditation on the day before, the day after, or the day of the full moon to connect to this vibration of Sacred Feminine energy as it holds the earth in its song.

Exercise: Receiving the gift of energy from the Moon Mothers

You can receive the gift of Sacred Feminine energy from the Moon Mothers at any time of day and as many times as you wish over the **three days of the full moon** – the day before the full moon, the day of the full moon and the day after the full moon.

You may like to choose a playlist of music and some incense and perfume that you feel is especially appropriate for the full moon.

1. Sit comfortably with your womb bowls. Place a lit candle in one bowl and drinking water in the other bowl.
2. Place a shawl around your shoulders to create a sacred female space and to help you to focus within.
3. Read or listen to the Womb Blessing meditation.
4. Sit relaxed and open to receive the beautiful Sacred Feminine vibration of the Blessing energy that is singing in the world.
5. When you are ready to end the meditation, take a deep breath, wiggle your fingers and toes, and open your eyes.
6. Offer your gratitude to the Sacred Feminine and to the Moon Mothers sending the energy. Drink your womb bowl water, then have something nice to eat.

Chapter 7:
The female archetypes and the Womb Blessing

At first, First Woman felt good that she had given her powers to Fox. She felt level, constant and predictable. She no longer heard the voices of the First Animals or met the Earth Mother when she cooked and cleaned. She no longer visited the animal clans or spoke with Moon Mother.

As the months came and went, her empty bowl moved within her belly in pain and cried out to Moon Mother for help. Angry, First Woman bound a cloth tightly around her belly and hips so that she would not hear the cries, and after a while it was quiet.

First Woman sat in the silence and knew that she was lost. The cry had been her last guide to returning home.

Walking the path of female development

Receiving the Sacred Feminine energy in a Womb Blessing attunement starts a process that awakens deeper aspects of our female archetypes and reconnects us more fully with their associated energies.

After the Womb Blessing we journey through the four phases of our menstrual cycle, and the Blessing energy continues to heal and awaken aspects of our true nature as it integrates with each of the archetypes associated with the phases. If we do not have a menstrual cycle, the Blessing energy integrates with each of the archetypes in association with the lunar phases. In both cases this allows the gifts of the archetypes to flow into our lives to be accepted, loved – and, most importantly, expressed.

The Womb Blessing is not something that we receive once and then we are 'fixed' – it is a path of transformation, growth and healing. Each attunement releases a layer of grime that hides the true form and vibrancy of our authentic femininity hidden underneath. However, **it is not enough just to awaken and restore our archetypes – they**

need to be lived or we will dim their colours again and lose the pattern of who we truly are.

If we fight our body and our cycle by ignoring our cyclic energies, then we resist the awakening and healing that the Blessing brings us, and we may return to our previous state of disconnection with its accompanying feelings of loss and incompleteness. Our path as women is not to live in the high ideals of the mind but to bring the light and love of the Sacred Feminine into the material world so that all everyday activities are sacred.

To help us through any resistance and to embrace the four archetypes, we need to actively nurture their energies within us and to live a creative and expressive life in harmony with them.

> **Receiving the Womb Blessing is like**
> **planting a rosebush and looking after it.**
> **Each Blessing helps the rosebush to**
> **grow deeper roots and reach higher towards the light.**
> **We then need to nurture this growth,**
> **allowing the rosebush to flow with the seasons,**
> **to grow wonderful buds and flowers,**
> **to develop healthy leaves and thorns,**
> **and to fill with beautiful red fruit.**

We can actively nurture our growth into full femininity by living as much as possible in tune with our archetypal energies and cyclic nature, or with the lunar cycle.

What are the archetypal energies? Our authentic femininity

Every woman holds four universal aspects of the Sacred Feminine energy, known as 'female archetypes', in her womb centre. The energies of the archetypes originate from our female soul within the womb centre and flow with the phases of our menstrual cycle, or the cycle of the moon, creating a personal experience of the universal rhythms of the Sacred Feminine.

Our authentic femininity with its four energies, four archetypes, and four levels of awareness want to be expressed – in our body, in our cells, in our instinct, and in our soul we are called to do this.

If the Womb Blessing attunement is awakening aspects of these archetypes within us and releasing their energies into our consciousness then **we need to know more about them**. We need to know how to recognise their presence and energies, and to discover what they require and how we can live with them in a balanced way. **By acknowledging and exploring the archetypal energies we are supporting each Womb Blessing and nurturing our path of change and awakening.**

Modern Life: No room for archetypes!

With the archetypes being repressed or ignored for thousands of years it is little wonder that modern women feel lost, and are seeking to understand themselves and the true place of femininity in the world.

But it is not ignorance that stops women from embracing their feminine energies. Even when they are given information about the female archetypal energies, many women are unable to empathise with the concepts or to apply them to their own lives. Sadly, it is women's state of separation from their body and femininity, influenced by a disconnected society, which leaves them unable to realise authentic femininity. 'I'd rather die young than grow old' and 'I hate my menstrual cycle, give me a pill to stop it' are attitudes that are symptoms of this separation. But the large positive response to the Worldwide Womb Blessing is also a symptom. The response of so many women from so many different countries and cultures shows that, regardless of their background, there is a core experience of femininity missing from their lives – and there is a heartfelt need to awaken this experience and to be free to be fully female.

Even if we feel that we are already connected to our female energies, the pressures and stresses of living a masculinised life means that we can easily become disconnected from the strength and wisdom our changing nature offers us. Stress and fear can swamp our consciousness, activating primal fear patterns and making it difficult for us to feel the subtle changes in our energies and consciousness.

It can be challenging for us to feel the changing flow of creativity and intuition, and hard to feel the beautiful and interactive relationship we have with the Sacred Feminine. The Womb Blessing is a gift of restoration, returning us back to who we are. It reminds us that we are safe, that it is safe to be open and flowing and feminine, and it reminds us that:

**Our strength lies not in what society
tells us and teaches us,
but what we feel in our womb centre,
in our heart,
in our phases
and in our connection to the Sacred Feminine.**

When we acknowledge the female archetypes of our cycle we see that there are no good or bad aspects of being female, but simply 'active' and 'receptive' energies. We also discover that there are aspects of our female archetypes that we deliberately repress or over-identify with, and that we are more than just one or two aspects of femininity but rather the wonderful blend of four archetypes that ebb and flow around the cycle.

Sadly, the world does not yet acknowledge the 'Cyclic Woman' and the positive gifts of the menstrual cycle, but:

**if we make small steps towards living
parts of our lives in tune with the archetypes
as they appear in our cycles
we will experience feelings of happiness, well-being,
completeness and fulfilment, because
we are expressing our true self.**

Meeting the archetypes: Looking in the mirror

My book Red Moon introduced the concept of four female archetypes related to a menstrual tradition. This concept emerged from the common experiences of women and the exploration of folklore and mythology for women's ancient wisdom passed down through the centuries. It was these stories that revealed the nature of the 'Cyclic Goddess'.

The Cyclic Goddess is the cycle of the stars across the night sky. She is the cycle of the seasons, the cycle of the tides, the cycle of the moon and the cycle of life – and She is also the cycle of women. We find Her in stories of women who change – women who change from the old crone into the young beautiful maiden, or the young maiden cursed to be an old ugly woman. We find Her in stories of women who shape-change into animals or birds that represent the powers of the different phases of femininity. The narrative and meaning of many of these stories has often changed with time, but if we read them from the position of a 'Cyclic Woman' we see the Cyclic Goddess revealing Herself to us in four female archetypes: the **Maiden**, the **Mother**, the **Enchantress** and the **Crone**.

The Maiden is the young girl who is dynamic, independent, sexually desirable, 'pure' in the sense that she is authentic to her nature and untouched by the influence of others.

> Know that you hold within you
> the light of the Sacred Feminine.
> Whatever happens,
> whatever has happened,
> you hold Her pureness.
> Today take action in awareness of
> your light,
> your beauty and grace.

Based on 'Spiritual Messages for Women' by Miranda Gray

The Mother is the 'Good Mother', the fertile woman who is caring and self-less and who is abundant in love and the ability to nurture and provide for those around her.

> To walk the path of the Mother energies
> is to walk tall and strong
> connected to the earth,
> with a fulfilled womb,
> open arms
> and an open heart.
> To embody the Sacred Feminine
> is to care for the World

Based on 'Spiritual Messages for Women' by Miranda Gray

The Enchantress is the mature woman who is empowered, sexual, magical, wild and independent. She can also appear as the 'Dark Maiden' or a magical being, and she reflects the energies of a woman who is peri-menopausal or who is in the early years of post-menopause.

> You have the permission of the Sacred Feminine to be
> passionate,
> wild,
> and instinctual!

This is who She made you to be *right now*.
When you love this aspect of yourself
and give yourself permission
you no longer need to fight a world that says otherwise.

Based on 'Spiritual Messages for Women' by Miranda Gray

The Crone is the lone old woman, the ugly witch, the elder wise woman, and the ancient grandmother. She is the old woman whose focus is turned inwards, away from the everyday world and society and who stands silently at the portal between the worlds.

Reach out with your fingertips and touch the stars.
Sense in your heart the beat of life.
Feel the love that lies in everything.
You and the Sacred Feminine are one.

Based on 'Spiritual Messages for Women' by Miranda Gray

A female journey: Understanding the energies of your cycle

As we journey through our menstrual cycles each month, we embody the beautiful energies of each of the four archetypes. Our cycle does not have rigid barriers between the phases, just as there are no rigid barriers between the seasons or the tides, and the changes we experience occur gradually as we move through one phase to the next.

The phases of the archetypes are not purely biological – although they are linked to hormonal changes, they are based on personal experiences. The cycle we experience is the cycle that is correct for us in this moment, whether it is long or short, regular or irregular, quiet or disruptive. How we experience our empowering cycles varies from woman to woman and from cycle to cycle, and the number of days in each phase can vary. However, as a first step towards understanding our unique expression of femininity we can make some generalisations.

The pre-ovulation phase starts after the menstrual phase – for many women it can occur around cycle days 7 to 13, where cycle day 1 is counted as the first day of menstruation. During this pre-ovulation phase we naturally start to express the beautiful **Maiden** archetypal energies and to see the world through her eyes. As we move towards ovulation, her dynamic energies start to soften and change into the loving Mother phase which can be around cycles days 14 to 20.

After the release of our egg, the **Mother** energies can change gradually, or in some cases dramatically, into those of the magical **Enchantress** as we begin our journey through the pre-menstrual phase – around cycle days 21 to menstruation.

Finally, around the first appearance of our blood we enter the wise **Crone** archetypal phase where we stay in her withdrawn energy until we start our rebirth back into the world with the dynamic Maiden energies.

These cycle days are only a guideline, so it is important to listen to your body and feelings as they tell you when you move from one archetype to the next. For some women the Crone energies can appear a few days before menstruation, for others they appear a few days after bleeding has started. Some women experience 'transition days' where they feel a combination of energies, needs and gifts from both the phase they are leaving and the phase they are entering.

Each archetype affects the way we think, feel and act, and is an important and powerful aspect of our femininity. Each archetype offers us amazing energies and opportunities to create the world around us and to express the Sacred Feminine. Whether we are conscious or not of the influence of the archetypes, **we change**.

Exercise: Looking in the mirror – the four archetypes within you

Women are like the moon – we change a little every day, and it can be difficult to see these changes when we just compare one day with the next. But if we compare one week with the next, it is much easier to see the changes in the face of the moon and within ourselves.

Sit comfortably and relax.

Imagine that four women are standing in front of you.

One is young and beautiful, and full of dynamic energy, goals and dreams.

One is slightly older, gentle and caring, and full of selfless love.

One is mature and full of magical power, dynamic energy and inspired creativity.

One is elderly, wise and still, who looks at you with deep love.

Now imagine that these four women all look the same.

Now imagine that these four women all look like you.

You have found yourself.

This is who you are now,
who you were last week,
who you will be next week and the week after.

Sit in this awareness.

When you are ready to end this exercise, take a deep breath and open your eyes.

It is no wonder that women are confused. We are told that we are one single woman, when in fact we are at least four different women with different energies, needs, skills and perspectives.

It is also no wonder that men are confused. They think that they have only one woman in their lives!

The archetypes and the Worldwide Womb Blessing: Helping us to heal our archetypes

By raising women's vibration, each Worldwide Womb Blessing attunement releases the archetype blocks and restrictions common to the women taking part. This creates a **collective awakening** of dormant or repressed aspects of their four female archetypal energies. The process of awakening starts with the attunement and then continues to work on each individual archetype through the following month.

The Blessing restores our connection to the archetype's energies, which is frequently and repeatedly broken by modern living, and it also replenishes any energies that have been depleted by modern life. The Blessing brings us back into archetypal equilibrium and flow so we are once more balanced in our cycles and within our self.

Each Worldwide Womb Blessing has an additional focus of healing the patterns and energies of a specific archetype. This healing is linked to the season of the earth at the time of the worldwide attunement. The earth, like the moon, goes through four phases, which occur due to her tilt towards or away from the sun, and each of her phases are associated with an archetype's energy.

In the Worldwide Womb Blessing we connect to the earth through the womb-earth-womb link, creating a resonance between our womb and her energies to re-establish the original archetype pattern and vibration within the womb centre. Energy flows up into our womb, bringing healing to the way that archetype is expressed into the world through our body and menstrual cycle.

The archetype healing and the year of Blessings

Archetype	Associated season	Worldwide Womb Blessing	Archetype healing includes:
Maiden	Spring: increasing daylight.	Beginning of spring energies.	**Our perception of the world.** Our thoughts, behaviour, ego, actions, self-confidence, optimism, self-belief, self-worth, sexual pleasure and personal growth. Our pre-ovulation phase.
Mother	Summer: long days.	Beginning of summer energies.	**Our connection to the world.** Our emotions, emotional strength, love, compassion, practicality, speaking our heart, connection, relationships, sexuality and fertility. Our ovulation phase.

Enchantress	Autumn: decreasing daylight.	Beginning of autumn energies.	**Our power in the world.** Our subconscious, beliefs, memories, creativity, sexual blocks, restrictions and inhibitions, manifesting, ego, fears, survival patterns and female ancestors. Our pre-menstrual phase.
Crone	Winter: short days.	Beginning of winter energies.	**Our being in the world.** Our soul, letting go, forgiveness, spirituality, intuition, spiritual sex, inner wisdom and soul purpose. Our menstrual phase.
Cosmos	The shortest day.	Winter solstice.	**Our oneness with all.** Completeness, centredness, stillness, inner peace, balance and harmony. The whole menstrual cycle.

To focus on healing specific patterns of archetypal energy, there are additional Worldwide Womb Blessing Archetype Meditations. These actively help us to **interact with the archetypal energies and to go deeper into our healing and expression of them.** As we journey along the yearly Womb Blessing path, we experience the archetypal energies in alignment with Mother Earth and so the meditations we use are reversed in the northern and southern hemispheres. For women who live near the equator, they have a choice of which yearly cycle of meditations they wish to follow.

The archetypal meditations and associated Worldwide Womb Blessings

Worldwide Womb Blessing	Meditation	Description
Beginning of spring energies	Womb Renewal	Gently cleansing and releasing the old patterns we hold in our femininity and wombs.
Beginning of summer energies	Accepting our Sexuality	Embracing the beauty, sensuality and sexuality of our femininity whatever our age.
Beginning of autumn energies	Creating Abundance	Releasing our natural abundance and female creativity to create our dreams.
Beginning of winter energies	Healing the Mother Ancestors	Healing the patterns of our female lineage. When we bring healing to the past, we heal the present and the future.
Winter solstice energies	The Circle of Sisters	Connecting with all the women in the Womb Blessing family to bring healing to the world and to ourselves.

These meditations are accessible for women with or without a physical cycle. Access to all the text and instructions for additional meditations are provided after registering for the Worldwide Womb Blessing.

The Archetype Meditations can also be undertaken in association with the lunar cycle and with the menstrual cycle.

The Spring Maiden Meditation: Womb Renewal

Northern Hemisphere: February Blessing
Southern Hemisphere: August Blessing

The additional Archetype Meditation at the beginning of spring has the focus of gentle cleansing and renewal. The Blessing energy works with the Maiden archetype to help us to let go of the patterns, hurt and emotional baggage from the previous year that can lie in our femininity and in our womb energy centre. In this additional meditation we support the healing by focusing on releasing the things we no longer need and breathing purity, goodness, love and peace into our womb and into the world. We are then birthed into the year cleansed, healed and renewed.

With each spring Womb Blessing attunement the healing of the Maiden goes deeper, healing our thoughts and beliefs about ourselves and bringing us back to the core of who we are.

The Summer Mother Meditation: Accepting our sexuality

Northern Hemisphere: May Blessing
Southern Hemisphere: October Blessing

In the Worldwide Womb Blessing that takes place at the beginning of summer we use the additional Archetype Meditation to bring healing to our sensuality and to the beauty of the sacred sexuality that lies in all of us. As the Mother archetype restores her energies and we reconnect with her aspects within us we begin to recognise our beauty and our desirability. We feel the sacredness and worth of our creativity, not just as fertile mothers but as creative sensual beings that give birth to ideas and create love and joy.

The summer Womb Blessing energy works with the Mother archetype to heal any limiting patterns and fears that we have learned from our own mothers about our sensuality, our body, our sexuality and pleasure. It also offers the intimate healing of our sexuality – physically, mentally and emotionally – and helps us to see our sexual nature as 'good' **in all its forms** and a reflection of the Sacred Feminine. The energy helps us to understand that all acts of loving pleasure are the prayers and rituals of the Sacred Feminine.

The Autumn Enchantress Meditation: Manifesting our abundance

Northern Hemisphere: August Blessing
Southern Hemisphere: February Blessing

In the autumn Worldwide Womb Blessing we work with the Enchantress meditation to bring healing to our sense of lack of abundance and to heal our inner needs. In a world where we are inundated with new things we 'should' buy or have, the sense of lack is easily enhanced, causing our inner Enchantress to respond as if we are threatened.

With the additional Archetype Meditation we soothe our sense of lack and centre ourselves once again in our – authentically female – power to manifest. With each autumn Womb Blessing the healing of the Enchantress restores our ability to create and manifest the life we desire through love and through the flowing of the energies of the Sacred Feminine. We remember that our nature is to be happy and that all actions taken from a feeling of love will bring us completeness, fulfilment and love.

The Winter Crone Meditation: Healing our female line

Northern Hemisphere: October Blessing
Southern Hemisphere: May Blessing

The Worldwide Womb Blessing at the beginning of winter focuses on healing and restoring the Crone energies that have become depleted. As the Crone heals we reconnect to our inherent inner peace and, accepting love, reunite with our inner wisdom and restore our bleeding time to sacredness.

We use the Archetype Meditation to support the Blessing energies in healing our maternal lineage, the ancestral past and group memory. None of us exists in isolation – we are the product of thousands of generations of mothers linking us back into the distant past. The Blessing energy flows back through the mother-womb to mother-womb connection, healing, cleansing and dissolving anything that is not in keeping with our new awakening. As the past heals, we heal, and so the present and future heal as well.

Oneness Meditation: The circle of sisters

Northern Hemisphere: December Blessing
Southern Hemisphere: December Blessing

The last Worldwide Womb Blessing of the year occurs around the time of the solstice, and we use the additional Oneness Meditation to support the Blessing's healing of our soul level consciousness and our connection to all women through our wombs and through our shared female experiences. The Blessing works with the centre of our cycle, the place **where all four archetypes merge into one conscious being that is the expression of the Universe through the feminine form**.

The Oneness Meditation helps us to feel part of the wider family of women, all connected through love and through our reflection of the Sacred Feminine. Each year it helps us to heal our feelings of loneliness and alienation, of confusion and fear, and it restores our loving strength and the awareness of all women being our sisters.

To take part in each Worldwide Womb Blessing and each Archetype Meditation is a beautiful spiralling path of healing and growth, remembering and restoration, and of love and evolution. It is an experiential path of loving our femininity and celebrating all its forms, and of growing in our awareness of our cycle and our connection to the cycles of the Sacred Feminine.

Your cycle phase and the Womb Blessing

In the Womb Blessing attunement the vibration of Sacred Feminine energy does not change with our menstrual cycle, but **our experience** of the Womb Blessing can change depending on the archetype that we are embodying at the time.

Receiving in our Maiden phase

If we receive the Worldwide Womb Blessing or a Personal Womb Blessing in our Maiden phase we may experience higher levels of awareness, a universal view of life, and more clarity and optimism – and we may be inspired to take action. After the attunement we may feel more self-confident and full of physical energy, wanting to move, to run or to dance.

Receiving in our Mother phase

Receiving the Womb Blessing attunement in our Mother phase can bring us deep feelings of love, helping us to relax the stresses of the world and to reconnect to the love that embraces the Universe. After the attunement we can feel emotional and loving, and may want to hug or touch people to share this love.

Receiving in our Enchantress phase

In our Enchantress phase the Womb Blessing attunement can bring us a deeper spiritual experience – we can feel more intuitive, receive inner knowledge or inspiration, and be more aware of the energy and its changes within us. We can also feel very emotional as deep feelings come to the surface to be released.

After the Blessing we can feel inspired and dynamic, with our wild side wanting to be released, or we can feel quiet and sit still in the emotions and spiritual experiences that we have received.

Receiving in our Crone phase

The Crone phase can give us a very deep and spiritual experience of the Womb Blessing. It can bring feelings of peace, love and acceptance, and a profound meditative experience of oneness. We may fall asleep or be close to sleep during the Blessing. After the attunement we can feel the oneness continuing so that we don't wish to move or speak.

The joy of the Worldwide Womb Blessing is that no two attunements are experienced in the same way. They are a beautiful combination of the stage of our personal energy development with our current cycle archetype, the archetype of Mother Earth, and the energy of the full moon. We are always given what we are ready to receive, and each Blessing brings us something truly beautiful and amazing even if we are unaware of it at the time.

**Each time we receive the Blessing,
we receive something new.**

Chapter 8:
Embracing the archetypes within you

To live more in harmony with the archetypes in our cycles between Womb Blessings, we need to understand who they are and how their energies affect our lives.

Meeting the Spring / Waxing Moon Maiden

Once the snows of winter had melted and the first shoots began to appear, Spring Maiden met First Woman, who was washing her blankets in the river.

Spring Maiden carried a bow and arrows, and two hounds stood by her. In her hair she wore a white flower – the same as the one that the Hare clan had given First Woman.

'Why are you so unhappy?' enquired Spring Maiden.

'Because I have lost something' said First Woman, 'and I don't know what it is.'

Spring Maiden saw that the bowl in First Woman's lower belly was empty of her power, and looked sad.

'I know what is missing' she said, and she handed First Woman back the flower that Hare Woman had given her at the making of the world. 'You gave this to Fox'.

First Woman jumped for joy and thanked Spring Maiden for returning her power, and she placed it on her belt.

Spring Maiden laughed.

'Stop doing your chores and run with me!' Spring Maiden said as she turned and started running.

First Woman felt the sluggishness of winter fall from her shoulders and a new energy vibrate in her bowl.

'Yes!' she cried, and together with the hounds, Spring Maiden and First Woman ran.

They dashed through the forest, leapt across rivers, ran over mountains and through the valleys beyond. First Woman felt alive and free, powerful and beautiful, and she created her own path as she ran.

The Maiden archetype: The journey begins

The Maiden archetype holds the energy of new beginnings, of movement and action, and of initial growth. She is the first buds of the growing season and the rushing water of the incoming tide. She is the sun starting its climb into the sky at dawn. She enters our lives in the pre-ovulation phase and with the increasing moon.

The Maiden phase of the cycle is one of renewed physical energy after the withdrawal and winter hibernation of menstruation. Our body feels lighter, our sexual interest and energies are renewed, our mind feels clearer, and we feel more confident and independent. The Maiden is unafraid of change and is willing to create a new path for herself in life. She is the goddess of the hunt who sets her goals and chases after them. She is full of positive energy about who she is and what she can manifest in her life.

In the Maiden phase our 'thinking mind' becomes dominant. The energies of our womb centre flow up to our mind, creating a strong mind-womb link.

The Maiden is the goddess of wisdom and intellectual knowledge. She is logical and rational, and open to intellectual ideals rather than empathic or intuitive approaches. In this phase our memory and concentration levels can be enhanced, as well as our desire to explore and learn.

The Maiden phase is also a phase of being true to ourselves, of simple joys and playful interaction with the world. The Maiden asks us for freedom from the responsibilities of the adult world and to enjoy a sense of fun.

The balanced Maiden

When the Maiden energies are balanced in our lives we are more able to achieve our dreams and goals and to meet our needs for growth and achievement, easily and without force. But when we live out of balance with her energies by suppressing her needs or by over-identifying with her energies, we can become frustrated and jealous of

101

other people's achievements or become un-empathic and let our work and personal goals dominate our lives.

Accepting the Maiden's energies

Many women love the Maiden energies. They enhance our abilities to succeed in our goal-orientated competitive society, and many women try to live only as the Maiden.

Other women can find the Maiden phase hard to accept. They can feel guilty about their self-orientated feelings because society has offered them an image of a 'good' woman as being selfless, nurturing and empathic *all the time*. However, if we allow ourselves the independent and self-determining expression of the Maiden energies, we feel more in control of our lives, we feel that we are growing rather than stagnating, and we feel empowered to be caring and generous.

Women can also find it hard to let their inner Maiden nature express itself through play and fun because of the burden of responsibility that comes from being a mother and from having a stressful job. Yet play is a way for us to release stress, to learn and grow, and to build empathic and loving relationships with our children.

Maiden creativity

The Maiden also offers us her uniquely expressed creativity, sexuality and spirituality. Her creativity is expressed through our intellect, giving us the wonderful ability to create structure out of chaos and to plan for the future.

Maiden spirituality

The Maiden's spirituality calls us to spiritual ideals, to ascension or enlightenment, and it creates a passion for rules, hierarchical structure, reasons, and ethical and moral practices. But we need to be aware that this path should be walked with her energies of playfulness if we are not to become obsessed with adhering to a strict, or 'right', regime.

Sex and the Maiden

The Maiden's sexuality is independent, and sex has no other purpose than to feel good and to be fun.

Mother Nature gives us this time before an egg is released to enjoy ourselves! For some women this phase can feel wonderful – their sexual energies have once again become dynamic after the withdrawal at menstruation, their body feels more alive, they feel self-confident and positive, and because their physical stamina is stronger late nights of passionate sex are a possibility.

Some women can, however, find this sudden dynamic sexuality difficult to manage, and for partners it can be a shock to go from living with a menstrual woman who is asleep most of the time and uninterested in sex to a pre-ovulation phase woman who wants to party, flirt and have wild sex.

Embracing the Maiden within us – whatever our age

When balanced, the Maiden energies are a beautiful gift of new beginnings, independence, vitality and playfulness. In order to balance these energies we need to actively embrace and express our 'thinking mind' abilities in planning activities, creating structure and learning something new. We need to embrace our self-confidence to begin new things, and to enjoy our renewed vitality by going out and being more physically active. But we also need to remember to embody the Maiden's tempering qualities of playfulness, flexibility and fun.

Whatever our physical age we are the Maiden; if we are cyclic we become the young girl once a month in our pre-ovulation phase, if we are post-menopause we hold her energies within ourselves to embrace with the increasing moon, with the spring, or whenever we choose.

The Womb Blessing and healing the Maiden phase

The Blessing can help us to release the old thought patterns that hold us back and that hide our heartfelt goals and dreams and our sense of who we truly are. Women receiving the Womb Blessing attunement in this phase can often feel energised afterwards, wanting to make big changes and to step onto a new path in life. The Blessing opens them to a self-confident, independent and dynamic aspect of themselves.

During our cycle of birthing after a Womb Blessing attunement the Blessing energy works with the Maiden archetype in our pre-ovulation phase to release us from restrictive and limiting thoughts and memories. We can rediscover our inherent goodness, re-awaken our sense of being beautiful and perfect just the way we are, and feel joy at being female. We become positive and empowered to take the steps we need to change our lives and allow our soul to walk its purpose in the world.

To live and work more consciously with the awakening and healing of the Maiden archetype in the month after the Blessing, see Chapter 9.

Exercise: Expressing the Moon Maiden energies

The key to living a more consciously authentic female life is to undertake activities in your phase that express your phase archetype and that make you feel happy.

This is a thinking exercise, because the 'thinking mind' is dominant in the Maiden phase.

If you are receiving the Womb Blessing attunement in your Maiden phase you may like to include this meditation in the remaining days of your phase.

> In your Maiden phase think about all the tasks and activities you want to do, or have to do, this week. The Maiden loves a list of jobs as it gives her direction, purpose and an outlet for her dynamic energies. Include some tasks that require concentration and clear thinking so that you use the Maiden's gifts.
>
> As you complete tasks, cross them off the list and you will notice that you feel good. The Maiden also loves to achieve things!

Meeting the Summer / Full Moon Mother archetype

The season changed from spring into the warmth of summer, and First Woman felt unbalanced. She had some of her power back, but not all, so she set out on a journey to find her missing powers.

At the Making of the World it had been easy to walk with the powers on her belt, but without all of them to balance her, her back ached and her feet hurt, and she became tired quickly.

After a long journey First Woman sat exhausted in the shade of a large tree. Summer Mother found her, and slowly sat down next to her. She was heavily pregnant.

'Ah daughter,' said Summer Mother, 'are you all right my little one?'

'Oh Mother,' cried First Woman, 'I have been tricked from my powers and I am lost and in pain.'

Summer Mother untied the bundle of reeds she carried, and started to weave a basket. As she wove she spoke to First Woman about the First Animals and their families and new babies. She spoke about their problems and their needs.

Before Summer Mother left in the early evening, she looked at her daughter's belt.

'I found this when I was looking for you' she said. 'It is the mirror that Horse Woman gave you at the Making of the World. Fox dropped it as he ran.'

In the morning, First Woman found that all the baskets woven by Summer Mother were full of the things the animals needed, and she picked them up and took them to share with her animal friends.

The Mother archetype: Reaching fullness

The Mother archetype is the energy of fullness, wholeness, poise and outward radiance. We find her in the fragrant blossoms of summer and the abundance of nature, and in the gentle light of the full moon. She is the stillness of the high tide, the warmth of the sun at noon, and the nurturing and caring energies of the ovulation phase.

The Mother reaches out to others in compassion and empathy to create relationships. She is the earth goddess giving birth to her children and nurturing them in their growth. The dynamic energy of the Maiden has softened, and the drive for action and self-determination has matured into an emotional strength that allows us to give and to care for others.

The Mother phase of ovulation and the full moon enables us to stand in our heart and to love our self, humanity, the earth and all living things. The Mother is rooted deep into the earth, giving her the strength and stability to open her heart, to love and care for others, and to give generously.

In the Mother phase our dominant way of thinking is our 'feeling mind' and the energies of our womb centre flow up to our heart, creating a strong heart-womb link. The Mother turns our awareness away from the intellect and towards the deeper level of flowing feelings where we experience empathy, understanding and compassion. We are no longer driven to personal achievement, but instead we feel contentment and fulfilment in being who we are and in caring for the needs and desires of others.

Balance and the Mother energies

Many women love this phase because it can feel so loving and giving. For many cultures it is the ideal image of what womanhood should be. But when the Mother is out of balance through our over-identification with her energies, we can give too much of ourselves by sacrificing our own needs for the needs of others – by offering disproportionate help when it's not really required and by taking on excessive responsibility. We forget that in the next two phases of our cycle our energy and stamina will decline and we will no longer be the person who can support others at this level.

If we try to embody the Mother energies all the time we miss out on growing the self, on attaining our higher levels of consciousness, and on creating the world in many different ways.

When we live out of balance with the Mother energies by suppressing her in our lives we can feel alone and less able to create mutually supportive relationships, and we can be unable to feel that emotional strength which brings generosity of the heart.

Accepting the Mother energies

Some women can have difficulties welcoming the Mother energies. They can fear losing the dynamic 'edge' that makes them successful in their lives and worry about losing themselves to others in the softer, more nurturing energies of the Mother. A dysfunctional relationship with their own mother can also give women a negative or distorted image of the Mother archetype, making them reluctant to fully embrace this aspect of themselves.

Mother creativity

Creativity comes in endless forms, and the Mother's creativity is with her hands, her heart and her womb. She gives us the gift of being more empowered to create feelings of love and harmony, and to support our wider network of friends, work colleagues and community. She enables us to create connections with others, to understand through our feelings, to communicate easily from the heart, and to create abundance and growth through nurturing.

Mother spirituality

For many women the Mother phase brings a strong connection to nature and a delight in the sensual experiences of the natural world. This is expressed in the Mother's inherent spirituality of simple truths, of a simple life, and of loving, helping and appreciating all life.

Sex and the Mother energies

Mother Nature can give us a wonderfully strong sexual energy in this phase that is deeply sensual and emotional. She asks us to open completely to our partner, emotionally and physically, and to share our body and heart. The Mother phase is about physical passion and romance, and about feeling loved, supported and validated by someone we feel we know at a soul level and who is committed to us.

Many women find this phase passionate, loving and giving, but when these aspects are suppressed we lose the beautiful opportunity to merge completely with our partner through love. Some women also find it hard to trust men enough to accept the openness of this phase and the vulnerability that comes with it. Other women hold back from the energies of this phase because they connect the Mother's sexuality with the risk of unwanted pregnancies.

Embracing the Mother within us – whatever our age

When accepted and balanced, the Mother energies bring us a phase of loving and physical caring, and of creation and abundance through allowing and nurturing. To balance her energies we need to embrace our 'feeling mind', let go of the drive of the Maiden, and merge with the Mother's ability to love and empathise. We need to reach out to people, show them in simple words and actions that we care, and take action to grow more harmonious relationships. We can also embrace her nurturing energies to help to empower projects to stand on their own when our energies decline in the Enchantress phase.

Whatever our age, whether or not we have children, we embody the Mother.

The Womb Blessing and healing the Mother phase

The Blessing's energy releases and heals our trapped feelings of pain and hurt, and it heals the scars that have closed our heart over the years. It clears the blocks that have stopped us loving and accepting ourselves, that stop us from trusting people and the Divine, and that are a barrier to intimacy and love.

Women receiving the Womb Blessing attunement in this phase can often feel tearful, gentle and caring, and want to hug those they are with to express their feeling of deep love for all things.

During our birthing after the attunement, the energies work with the Mother archetype to bring healing to our heart, to our relationships and to our fears, and to give us the emotional strength to be open and vulnerable to the world. We can rediscover the inner calm and peace that comes with self-acceptance and feel whole and complete. We can also feel deep compassion and love arise in our lives, allowing us to make sacrifices to support others.

To live and work more consciously with the awakening and healing of the Mother archetype in the month after the Blessing see Chapter 9.

Exercise: Embracing the Full Moon Mother energies

This meditation helps us to connect to the Mother energies, and is based on one from *Red Moon*. Our Mother archetype is strongly linked to nature, and she experiences the world through her sensuality and feelings. This is a feeling meditation because our 'feeling mind' is dominant in the Mother phase.

If you are receiving the Womb Blessing in your Mother phase, you may like to include this meditation in the remaining days of your phase.

> Sit in a garden or somewhere you can see a view of trees and plants.
>
> Notice the vibrancy of the colours, the depth of the shadows and the brilliance of the sunlight.

Now imagine, know or feel that the landscape merges into the beautiful garment of the Mother Earth. Recognise yourself as part of her garment and feel her presence around you.

Feel around you the peace and inner harmony she brings, and from deep within you feel love bubble up like a spring. All life around you is connected in the warp and weft of her garment, and it shimmers with the creative energies which radiate from her.

Become aware of these creative energies within yourself, connecting you with all life. Feel it pulse in your heart and in your hands with the need to reach out and nurture and care.

Allow these energies to spread beyond you, your own needs no longer important as you feel the desire to comfort, to protect, and to help heal and soothe the pain of others.

Rest in the energies of the Mother.

When you are ready, bring your awareness gently back to your surroundings. Feel love and peace for everything that you see and take these feelings out into your everyday life.

Meeting the Autumn / Waning Moon Enchantress archetype

When the trees started to turn yellow and orange, and the leaves started to fall, the beautiful mature Autumn Witch met First Woman gathering sticks for a fire.

Autumn Witch wore a cloak of raven feathers and small silvers bells that tinkled as she walked. Without talking, she helped First Woman to clear the ground of fallen branches and build a large fire.

With a graceful gesture her magic lit the fire, and then she began to dance, her feet drumming the heartbeat of the earth.

Well into the night First Woman and Autumn Witch wove together the wild magic of earth and air, fire and water.

A crescent of silver flashed as Autumn Witch danced, and in a swirl of laughter and light, she gave First Woman back the knife that Owl Woman had given her.

The Enchantress archetype: Stepping into darkness

The Enchantress archetype is the energy of change, of letting go, of wildness and spiritual awareness. She is the golden colours of the land as the life force withdraws in the autumn, the decreasing light across the face of the moon, and the swirling danger of the out-going tide. She is the declining sunlight and the growing darkness of twilight. As we journey from the ovulation phase to the pre-menstrual phase, the Enchantress brings these powerful energies to us.

The Enchantress phase is one of dancing down the steps into the welcoming darkness at the heart of the labyrinth. As the light from the outside world gradually vanishes, so does our physical, mental and emotional energy, and our dance becomes slower and an expression of our increasing spiritual awareness. Who we are as we dance the steps can be very different to who we are when we finally rest at the centre. In the darkness there is no light to guide us, only the hand of the Enchantress and her needs, intuition and magic. She is the beautiful mature witch, the enchanting seductress, the goddess of sex and magic and the goddess of challenge and change. She is beautiful, self-empowered, sexual, unrestricted and magical.

As with the other phases, we experience a dominant way of thinking in the pre-menstrual phase, and our Enchantress mind is dominated by our subconscious level of thinking and awareness. The Enchantress takes us beneath everyday thought into the magically creative world of the subconscious, and our womb energies stay centred and spiralling in our womb.

For many women this is the hardest phase, because they try to match the expectations of a world that doesn't acknowledge their descent, and as a result they live the effects of a neglected Enchantress. The image of the pre-menstrual woman as a harridan, who scolds and demands, challenges and threatens, who is fickle and nasty, and who is aggressive and angry, is an image of a woman who is not free to embrace her Enchantress energies. She is a woman who is unable to rest and withdraw, who is unable to give herself the nurturing she requires and who is threatened by ignorance of who she is and the incredibly creative and spiritual powers she embodies.

It is no wonder that many women hate who they are in this phase. Where symptoms break relationships and make survival difficult, women can escape this phase by blocking their cycle; but in doing so they lose their female energies to a society that is the cause of the problem and not the solution.

Balancing the Enchantress energies

To balance the Enchantress in our lives we need to accept our phase changes and to nurture ourselves through more rest and sleep and through creative and spiritual expression. The emotional reactions of the Enchantress can be hard to control because they come straight from the subconscious and occur before our rational brain realises.

When we deny our increasing need for rest and withdrawal, our primitive brain is more likely to see anything that is a drain on our energies as a threat – and we attack. When we suppress the Enchantress energies, our frustration can build, and feelings of inner emptiness, lack of power and lack of worth can grow.

Women who live in a threatening environment can often over-identify with the Enchantress because of the sense of self-empowerment that her extreme emotions can create. When we feel anger, we can feel powerful. However, when we express and nurture her energies and needs, we feel self-love – and through that love we feel empowered to make any changes that we need in our lives.

Accepting the Enchantress energies

Accepting the Enchantress is not always easy, especially if she is in an unbalanced state and creating wild mood swings, pain, uncomfortable physical symptoms, compulsive activity, and feelings of emptiness, isolation, anxiety, and deep and sudden withdrawal.

Many women are simply unable to slow down in the Enchantress phase due to the high pressures and expectations, and the deadlines and responsibilities, of their lives. And they fight any attempts by the Enchantress to make them withdraw and rest more until, exhausted after fighting an Enchantress who fights back even harder, they fix the problem with hormonal suppression.

For other women who lacked love, acceptance and validation in their childhood, the patterns in their subconscious use the Enchantress phase 'symptoms' to cry out their need for self-love and self-acceptance.

111

Some women, however, love their Enchantress phase because of the whirlwind of creative and sexual energy, the profound inspiration, and the deep spiritual connection and insight it brings. For those women who can rest more in the Enchantress phase, who can take time for creative and spiritual expression, and who are not scared to take the steps into the inner world, the Enchantress brings amazing gifts.

Enchantress creativity

The Enchantress gifts us with enhanced inspiration, impulsiveness, intuition, a need for clearing and space, and the magical power to manifest. She gives us a creativity that can be wild, driven and compulsive.

It is important for our peace and harmony in this phase to have a simple project to release her creative energies. The outcome of her creativity is not important – what is important is to meet her need to allow her creativity to flow into the world and experience the wild joy of this process.

Enchantress spirituality

The Enchantress stands between light and dark, between the inner and outer worlds, and between the manifest world and the spiritual. She brings us a desire to interact with the spiritual world, to bring oracle and guidance from the depths of our intuition, and to create the simple magic of the wise woman of herbs and nature as well as the ritual magic of the priestess.

Her spirituality is her own, free from rules and restrictions, and originates from her personal spiritual connection to the Sacred Feminine.

Sex and the Enchantress energies

The Enchantress also brings the magic of a naturally vibrant, sensual and erotic sexual energy. Originating in our dynamic journey down into the darkness, our sexual energy is an affirmation of life and a response to the release of inhibitions that chain our subconscious through the rest of the month. Enchantress sexuality can be more exotic, more sensual and more dominating than in any other phase, but it can also be expressed in vulnerability and in needing comfort and reassurance.

The Enchantress energies respond to our subconscious acceptance of our personal power, acceptance of ourselves, and our level of self-love. When we do not have self-acceptance and love, our sexual desire can become demanding and dominant, or needy and clingy. When we embrace our journey into the Labyrinth, love ourselves and meet our needs, we bring balance and love to the exciting and adventurous sexual energies of the Enchantress phase.

As we travel deep into the darkness we experience a gradual decline in physical energies, but within this decline we can experience multiple peaks of energy. At the beginning of the phase these peaks of dynamic energy may encompass the majority of the day, but as we journey deeper into the phase they reduce in length and strength and are accompanied by longer periods of low physical energy.

Finally, our peaks of vitality are gone, and we have entered the Crone energies of the next phase. This means that our desire for active participation in sex experiences decreasing peaks as this phase progresses, until the peak can simply be a brief recognition of sexual desire which is then lost within a few seconds!

Embracing the Enchantress – whatever our age

The Enchantress phase is one of turning away from everyday wants and needs and withdrawing to a deeper, more spiritual aspect of life. To balance her energies we need to embrace her magic, perhaps by creating little rituals out of everyday tasks – for example making wishes for health as we stir the pan of spaghetti. We need to give our subconscious more love by doing things that nurture us, and we need a way to release the Enchantress creativity and inspiration. But most importantly, in this world of activity and connection, we need time to withdraw and be alone with her.

Whatever our age we embody the magic of the Enchantress.

The Womb Blessing and healing the Enchantress phase

The Womb Blessing attunement can help us to release old memories, anger and frustration, and to recognise that beneath these patterns lies our lack of self-love and self-acceptance. The Blessing allows us to see the negative thoughts and actions of the pre-menstrual phase as messages showing us our lack of self-love and our neglect of the Enchantress phase in our lives.

113

During our birthing after a Blessing, the energies work with the Enchantress archetype to release our deep subconscious patterns, beliefs and memories, and to heal the negative emotions associated with them by changing these emotions into love and strength. The Enchantress brings us messages of fear so that we can see the path to love, and she creates a space for the Crone to bring transformation into our lives. The Blessing energy also helps us to rediscover our natural Enchantress spirituality, to re-awaken our intuitive inspiration and powerful creativity, and to feel joy in this phase.

Our Enchantress phase is one of naturally declining energies, and so it is important after the Womb Blessing attunement that we eat regularly and healthily and sleep more to give our body the resources it needs to support the energy changes. When we accept our declining energies and our natural withdrawal into a spiritual awareness of life, we return one step closer to our authentic femininity.

The Enchantress phase can be more intense after the Womb Blessing as she clears away the clutter from our lives to allow healing and new growth to occur. So we need to be gentle with ourselves, take time to nurture our body and emotions, and reduce or prioritise our activities, especially towards the end of the phase. Moon Mothers offer Female Energy Balancing which can be very supportive for this phase.

To live and work more consciously with the awakening and healing of the Enchantress archetype in the month after the Blessing see Chapter 9.

Exercise: Conjuring with the Waning Moon Enchantress energies

In the Enchantress phase we have the gifts of wild creativity and inspiration. Waving her wand, we imagine and make real whatever we want – which is why when we have a negative thought in this phase it looks and feel very real even if it is untrue!

In my book *The Optimized Woman* the subconscious mind, which is dominant in this phase, is compared to a puppy who will run after anything we throw for it. Our 'puppy mind' will then bring back what we throw, plus many other similar things it finds. To keep our eager puppy mind and our creative powers away from

---

the negative thoughts we throw, we need to give it something positive to play with instead.

The following exercise is based on one from *The Optimized Woman*. If you are receiving the Womb Blessing in your Enchantress phase, you may like to include this meditation in the remaining days of your phase.

> Pick a problem that needs solving, or something for which you want some guidance or inspired ideas.
>
> During the Enchantress phase, just allow your heightened subconscious to process the problem or topic. You do not need to do anything except be receptive to ideas, feedback and synchronicity.
>
> When you are actively interacting with the intuitive Enchantress powers and releasing her creativity into the world, you will feel good!

Ideas and synchronicity can come at any time, and in this phase of declining mental skills we can easily forget them, so carry a notebook with you to write down answers and ideas as they occur.

Meeting the Winter / Dark Moon Crone archetype

> The snow was deep on the ground when the Winter Old One found First Woman huddled by a small fire. The Winter Old One wore tattered cloth and skins, and leaned on a gnarled staff, smoking a pipe. Her face was full of deep lines, but her eyes sparkled with wisdom.
>
> They sat together watching the fire, and Winter Old One drew a drum from under her skins and warmed it in the fire's glow.
>
> After a while Winter Old One began to drum and to sing softly in a low voice. She sang of the Making of the World, of the making of First Woman, of the First Animals, of the Star People and of the deepness of space. She sang about the Universal Mother, of her love and spirit that fills all things. She sang about the Mother of Compassion and Love who holds the world in her warm embrace, and about the Earth Mother who clothes us in our bodies and fills us with life.

When she stopped, she drew out First Woman's obsidian bowl from under her skins and held it out to her.

'I would have brought it to you sooner' she apologised, 'but I am old and slow.'

With the four power objects returned to her belt, First Woman felt the bowl in her belly fill once again with the waters of life and the flame of creation.

The Crone archetype: Our journey's end

Although we can use our diary and the first signs of bleeding to help us to know when we may be changing into the Crone archetypal energies, it is our personal feelings that tell us when we have actually changed.

The Crone sits at the heart of the labyrinth and she is the energy of potential, of balance, stillness, hibernation, death and the Universe. She is the quiet stillness of winter, the withdrawn life force of hibernation, the hidden face of the moon, and the empty stillness of the low tide. She is the darkest moment of night before the dawn starts the day again. When she enters our lives at menstruation, she brings us depth and stillness.

The dominant thinking in the Crone phase is that of 'soul-thinking', which guides us through heartfelt feelings to know what is important for us and what is our purpose and direction in life. The energies of our womb centre flow down into the earth, creating a strong earth-womb link. The Crone is the ancient wise woman, the isolated old witch, the hidden goddess of the underworld, and the goddess of the souls and of rebirth.

The Crone gives us the opportunity to leave our emotional baggage behind. In the darkness at the heart of the labyrinth we can leave the emotions and experiences of the old month, and start the journey back out into the light feeling cleansed and reborn. The Crone also gifts us with enhanced insight and inner awareness, the increased ability to forgive and let go, and connection to a universal perspective. She helps us to commit to a new path and she shows us that we can be healed, forgiven, and given a second chance to do things better and in alignment with our soul's goodness.

Balancing the Crone

The Crone energies are balanced in our menstrual phase by resting more and by withdrawing. When we accept our slowness, our peaceful mind, and our lack of desires, we can feel spiritual oneness with the Universe and experience an inner knowing of the right decisions or direction for us to take.

If we suppress the Crone energies by forcing ourselves against her nature, the lack of time to heal and restore our energies in this phase can leave us tired and exhausted in our next Maiden phase and throughout the month. Without the Crone's involvement in our lives we can also feel a lack of purpose or direction.

For some women, the Crone phase offers them an escape from the everyday world, and their over-identification with the Crone energies makes their spirituality ungrounded and everyday life difficult to participate in.

Accepting the Crone energies

The Crone phase can be a major challenge for many women. For some there is a huge sense of relief that the chaotic physical, mental and emotional rollercoaster ride of the Enchantress has finished, but for many, especially those with jobs that require sharp intellectual skills and high levels of performance, this phase can seem disabling.

We live in a world fixed in the Maiden archetypal energies, and so it can be very challenging for women to let go and to accept the cyclic flow of their body and abilities. It can be emotionally difficult for us to withdraw and rest – we feel guilty that we are not being productive or that we are 'not good enough' if we are not matching the work hours of everyone else. These thoughts activate our survival instinct, and we can find ourselves either suppressing this phase to keep going, or feeling emotionally overwhelmed by the darkness that forces us to rest.

If we fight this phase we miss out on the restorative and healing powers of the Crone, we lack self-forgiveness, we do not hear the inner guidance of our soul, and we do not experience our inherent oneness with the Universe.

Crone creativity

The Crone is the potent power that creates the stars and the souls of all life. Her creativity lies in stillness and emptiness – a space held to be filled with an inner knowing, a gentle feeling and an intuitive wisdom beyond words. There is no need to outwardly express our creativity – we simply need to be still, to hold our intention within our heart and let its vibration flow out into the world to create our purpose.

Crone spirituality

The Crone has no desire for intellectual spirituality or interactive ritual and magical manifesting. Her spirituality lies in the oneness of being. Everyday life is a meditation, a prayer without words, and a loving interaction with the Sacred Feminine in all Her forms.

Sex and the Crone energies

The Crone's spirituality and sexuality are merged together in a sense of being. Many women do not experience a passionate desire for active sex in this phase, and this is misinterpreted as a lack of sexual energies.

The Crone phase offers us a sexual approach which brings together the feeling of letting go, of openness to the Universe, of love and trust, and a deep merging of souls. The feeling of being totally open and receptive with a partner in a mindful experience makes sex a prayer and a spiritual meditation on love.

Women who experience an active sexual desire in this phase can find it easier to reach orgasm or experience a deeper type of climax. Whether we are active or passive sexually, sex is a deep expression of the sensual merging of souls with the Divine.

Embracing the Crone energies – whatever our age

The Crone brings us the powerful and beautiful gift of a deep meditative state which creates soul connection, healing and restoration, and a natural acceptance of all things. By embracing her enhanced energies in this phase through stopping, resting, stillness meditation and letting the world carry on without us, we 'allow' life to happen without getting in its way. When we do this, the Sacred Feminine takes over and magic happens in our body and in our life.

The Crone offers us the amazing gift of the ability to be renewed every month and to take her wisdom out into the world of light.

Whatever our age, we embody the energies of the old wise Crone and we stand with one foot in the mundane world and one foot amongst the stars.

The Womb Blessing and healing the Crone phase

The Womb Blessing attunement enables us to become more aware of the Crone energies of stillness and spiritual connection and to accept that they have a benefit and a purpose in our lives. It helps us to see the importance of rest in our menstrual phase as the way for us to connect with this aspect of our self. The Blessing also releases negative patterns surrounding our bleeding, not just from our own upbringing and experiences but also from our ancestral lineage. It helps us to reclaim the sacredness of our blood and our time of bleeding, to enjoy the gifts of the Crone, and to accept everything as it is with love – including ourselves.

Women receiving the Womb Blessing attunement in this phase can often experience strong visions, guidance and knowledge of their purpose in life. After the attunement they can experience a need to be still and quiet, to do nothing or to sleep.

During our birthing after the Womb Blessing attunement, the energies work with the Crone archetype to release the deep blocks that cover our female soul pattern in order to allow the soul's energies and guidance to flow into our lives. We can awaken to the Crone's direction as she brings us into harmony with our soul and in alignment with the Sacred Feminine. We are empowered by deep transformation and rebirth, and we can rediscover the spiritual in the hustle and bustle of modern life.

The Womb Blessing can also bring the Crone phase to us earlier or later than expected in our cycle, increase or decrease the number of days that we bleed, or increase or decrease the amount we bleed. This occurs because our body's cycle is slightly altered with respect to the lunar cycle, making our ovulation and menstruation occur at a different phase of the moon.

The alignment of our menstruation with the lunar phases is a reflection of our current path and purpose in life. Sometimes when we don't listen to the Crone our purpose and our cycle orientation become misaligned. The Blessing returns our cycle to its authentic alignment.

We can view this as a wonderful sign of the energy that is healing and transforming both our body and our life.

To live and work more consciously with the awakening and healing of the Crone archetype in the month after the Blessing see Chapter 9.

Exercise: Celebrating the Dark Moon Crone energies

The Crone energies can often be at their strongest during the first two or three days of bleeding. During this time it is important that we rest to restore our body's energy and that we take time to meditate and daydream to connect with the Crone's wisdom and our soul's desires.

The three meditations below are designed to help you to connect to your dominant soul-level thinking in this phase. If you are receiving the Womb Blessing in your Crone phase, you may like to include these meditations during your phase.

For the first three days of bleeding, light a candle and read the corresponding message from the Sacred Feminine below.

Relax and allow the words to sink into your being. Hear the truth of them resonate in your bones.

Relax even deeper and feel the love and the wisdom of the Crone within you.

Know that in this time and space you touch the face of the Sacred Feminine.

First day of bleeding:

The presence of the Sacred Feminine lies
in stillness and inner awareness.
Every expression of being, every moment of silence,
every act of inner awareness,
is a prayer connecting you with the Sacred Feminine.

Second day of bleeding:

Forget what others expect from you now.
You rest at the heart of the labyrinth.
Only the voice of the Sacred Feminine is important.

Third day of bleeding:

By dwelling in the presence of the Sacred Feminine we are changed.
Not from the top down, but from the depths out into the light.
Rest now, in the darkness of the Sacred Feminine, and change.

These messages are based on ones from *Spiritual Messages for Women* by Miranda Gray.

A quick guide to the archetypal energies and associations

Our relationship with our cyclic nature, with our female energies and with the Sacred Feminine are personal to us, but there are many experiences of our cyclic energies that we have in common with other women.

The Sacred Feminine is not about rules and regulations but about creativity, exploration and play. We can use other women's experiences and ideas as *inspiration*, and then explore our own unique cycle and relationship with the Divine Feminine.

Maiden archetype	Mother archetype	Enchantress archetype	Crone archetype
Pre-ovulation phase	**Ovulation phase**	**Pre-menstrual phase**	**Menstrual phase**
Increasing moon	Full moon	Decreasing moon	Dark moon
Spring	Summer	Autumn	Winter

Growth / Bud	Abundance / Flower	Decline / Fruit	Withdrawal / Hibernation
Outward energy	Outward energy	Inward energy	Inward energy
Young girl	Fertile woman	Peri-menopausal woman / Woman in early active years of post-menopause	Elder woman / Woman in passive years of post-menopause
Flower Maiden	Earth Mother	Beautiful mature witch / Enchantress	Ancient wise woman / ugly witch
Growth and wonder	Maturing and experience	Challenge, transformation	Restoration, gestation, and rebirth
White, yellow, bright green	White, pink, deep green	Intense purple, black, deep blue	Black, red, brown, deep purple
Lady of purity	Lady of compassion	Lady of miracles	Lady of the grotto
Mental mind dominant	Feeling mind dominant	Subconscious mind dominant	Soul mind dominant
Dynamic sex / Playful sexual acts	Abundant sex / Emotional sexual acts	Erotic or 'needy' sex / Magical sex	Spiritual sex / Passive sexual acts
Idealistic / Intellect-based spirituality	Love / People-based spirituality	Magic / Earth-based spirituality	Universal / oneness-based spirituality

Write lists / Structure and plan	Cook / Make things	Paint inspired pictures / Write intuitive poetry / Dance	Day-dream / Listen to your heart and soul
Starting projects	Supporting projects	Reviewing projects	Rest and reflection

Exercise: The archetypes and their intimate energy points

In a *Womb Healing – Female Energy Balancing*, Moon Mothers work with the archetypal energy points that form a grid or gateway within the receiver's womb energy centre in order to restore and balance their energies. The healing creates a balanced connection and flow between the archetypes to bring harmony to our cycle or to ease the process of merging during our journey into post-menopause.

There is another more intimate set of energy points that we can use in a self-healing to help to energise the archetypes and in particular their sexual vibration.

The meditation uses a long slow in-breath and a relaxed out-breath.

Sit comfortably upright, or lie down for this meditation.

Bring your awareness to your clitoris. As you slowly breathe in energy from the earth, say in your mind 'Maiden'.

Breathe out slowly.

Bring your awareness to your G-spot inside the entrance to your vagina. Slowly breathe in, saying in your mind 'Mother'.

Bring your awareness to your cervix – the entrance to your womb. Slowly breathe in, saying in your mind 'Enchantress'.

Breathe out slowly.

Bring your awareness to your womb and ovaries. Slowly breathe in, saying in your mind 'Crone'.

Breathe out slowly.

Let the energy rest in your womb and ovaries as you breathe normally.

Repeat the breath sequence several times.

Practising this meditation can make orgasm easier or change the experience we have at orgasm, especially if we are peri-menopausal or post-menopause.

Cycles within cycles: Combining archetypal energies

The Moon Above and the Moon Within

The menstrual cycle is one of most impactful influences on adult women, and it affects all levels of their being. When we are not being dominated by stress responses, how we think, feel and behave can all be dominated by the current phase we are experiencing and the level of awareness and enhanced skills it offers.

But there is another influence which we all experience, and this is the effect of the moon. Some of us are very aware of the effect of the moon's cycle, especially if its phases coincide with our own cycle phases, as it can enhance our feelings and experiences. For example, the increasing moon is associated with the same Maiden archetypal energies as our pre-ovulation phase, and so when the two are combined we can feel heightened dynamic energies, stronger desires to start new things, and more intense feelings of renewal and rebirth. Ovulation at the time of the full moon can deepen our Mother feelings of gentleness, motherliness, compassion and empathy, while the decreasing moon can heighten the magic, intuition and spirituality of the Enchantress pre-menstrual phase. Finally the dark moon, withdrawn from the sky, enriches our own withdrawn Crone state at menstruation, taking us deeper into soul consciousness and Universal awareness.

Women whose cycle is not in synch with the lunar cycle or whose cycle is irregular, however, are given an amazing gift – the experience of different archetypal energies merging together. It's like a painter mixing paints to create new and exciting colours. These women embrace a rich palette of experiences born from the merging of their own archetype's energy and the different archetypal moon energy. For example, a woman in her Maiden phase at the time of the full moon can feel a softening of her Maiden energies and a more altruistic direction to her actions and goals.

A cycle not in synchronicity with the moon provides us with a wonderful multifaceted experience with unique inspiration and wisdom about the Sacred Feminine and more insight into the beautiful creativity and complexity that is woman.

Drumming seasons, dancing cycles

The seasons also influence how we feel during our cycles. The four seasons reflect the energies of the four phases of the moon and the energies of the four phases of the menstrual cycle.

Each season surrounds us with the energies of one of the four archetypes. If we are cyclic it can enrich our experience of the associated archetype within our own cycle. For example, the winter can enhance the withdrawn energies of our menstrual Crone phase, making us want to hibernate; the quickening life force of spring can heighten our impulse to be outgoing and dynamic in our pre-ovulation Maiden phase; the abundant energies of summer can open our hearts more in our ovulation Mother phase; and the wild energies of autumn can evoke strong feelings of being magical and creative in our pre-menstrual Enchantress phase.

The season also has an effect on the other phases in our cycle which are not directly associated with it. For example, the dynamic energies of the spring merge with the Crone energies of menstruation and we become a 'Dynamic Crone'. In the summer we are influenced by the energies of the Mother in the Earth to become the 'Loving Crone'. In our autumn menstruations we can express the 'Mystical Crone' and in the winter we once again return to the pure state of Crone at menstruation.

In climates such as deserts and mountains, and in sub-tropical zones, the land responds differently to the seasons compared to temperate climates. Local mythology and folklore, celebrations and rituals, and personal observations and intuition can guide us towards recognising the local archetypal energies. The exercises in this book can easily be adapted to work with the four temperate seasons and they can also be used as inspiration for women in other types of climate to create their own seasonal path of connecting with the archetypal energies.

Our cyclic experience is a beautifully complex and unique combination of Sacred Feminine energies. The influences of the cycles of the body, the moon and the earth are cumulative - for example, we may experience the 'Triple Crone' effect of menstruation at the dark moon in winter, or a 'Double Mother' effect of ovulation with the full moon. The archetypes are a fundamental part of our lives, whether or not we are aware of them, and together they bring us the opportunity for increased well-being and enhanced creativity and spiritual insight.

The archetypes and non-cyclic women

'Why would I be interested in the archetypes? – I have finished **my cycles!**'

It's strange how for many women the womb can become an unimportant and disregarded part of the body after their cycles stop. It is such a sad reflection of modern society that the wombs of mature women are seen as uninfluential in their lives, unless the journey into menopause created disruptive symptoms. But even if our wombs no longer have the potential to hold and grow a child, the womb energy centre is still within us and we still hold the four female archetypes and their energies. A Cyclic Woman expresses these archetypes through her cycle phases, but for the post-menopause woman the archetypal energies are an intrinsic part of who she is and the source of the 'magical' powers she holds.

What happens at menopause? Becoming complete

Imagine a four-sided lampshade where each side is a different colour. As Cyclic Women we journey around the outside of the lampshade, and life is coloured by the light from each side. We experience life through the perception and energies of the archetype of the phase we are travelling through. But when we are no longer cyclic we instead become the light bulb at the centre of the shade, where we contain all four colours in white light.

The four female archetypes represent the way we think and perceive the world. As Cyclic Women the dominant way we see the world changes as we travel though our different phases. As post-menopause women we have a very different opportunity – to stand at the centre of our awareness in a fifth state of womanhood, with all four archetypes embodied equally and merged into one. We become a Complete Woman – we embody the whole of our cycle, the whole of the moon's cycle, and the whole of the cycle of the seasons. We are complete within our being, holding the wisdom of the Crone, the vibrancy of the Maiden, the selfless love of the Mother and the magical creativity of the Enchantress.

How the Womb Blessing helps us to become Complete Women

The path of becoming a Complete Woman begins with peri-menopause and then continues on after the menstrual cycles have ceased. Sadly, many women are not able to achieve the full realization of this beautiful fifth state, because they still have unrealised aspects from their cyclic path. To blend a rainbow into white light, all the shades of colours need to be represented, clear, and balanced.

Living a life that is disconnected from our cyclic nature leaves aspects of the archetypes and their energies unaccepted and unexpressed. During the change from cyclic to non-cyclic femininity the archetypal aspects that haven't previously been fully embraced rise to the surface to be acknowledged and integrated into our being. We see this manifest in women entering post-menopause who may leave their partners or families for younger partners because they have not fully expressed the wild sexual energies of the Enchantress. We see it in women who suddenly decide to study for a University degree later in life because they have not fully realised the intellectual energies of the Maiden. Women also leave highly paid careers for vocational and caring work to express their restricted Mother archetype, or they travel the world exploring different spiritualities to express their dormant Crone spiritual energies.

The change to a Complete Woman can be a frightening and confusing path if we don't recognize the needs and energies of each archetype or how we can embody them gently and creatively without disrupting aspects of our life. Some women never totally evolve into Complete Women, even though their cycles ended many years ago, because aspects of their archetypes and energies have remained repressed by their culture and society, or by their beliefs and life experiences.

Confidence in peri-menopause and post-menopause comes with the **knowledge of the archetypal energies**, and empowerment comes from **recognising these energies when they appear** and **the ability to meet their needs**. Without a repeating cycle an archetype can be dominant for a number of weeks or even months. It can be dominant for a day, or we can experience two or more archetypes flowing through us in the same day!

Without an understanding of the archetypes we can feel like we are out of control and that who we are is collapsing. Once our menstrual cycle has become irregular or disappeared altogether, living more in tune with the *lunar* cycle can help us to create a loving relationship with each archetype, to ease the archetypal energies into our lives without fear and confusion, and to express our energies and gifts in everyday life. Connecting with our womb centre can also help us to acknowledge its presence as the amazing source of our female energies and the home to our female soul.

The Womb Blessing is as important for peri-menopausal and post-menopausal women as it is for Cyclic Women.

The Womb Blessing helps us to make the change from Cyclic Woman to Complete Woman in a way that is beautifully balanced, harmonious, self-accepting and empowering. We do not need to wait until the pressure of the archetype that needs to be released is so strong that it disrupts our life in the intensity of its desire to be expressed. Instead, each Womb Blessing awakens these aspects so that we can gently accept them and gracefully express them in little ways during our everyday lives.

The Womb Blessing helps us to release old patterns of fear and restriction from our own lives and from our female line, to awaken missing aspects of the archetypes, and to feel that the form of femininity we are becoming – or have become – is as wonderful, beautiful, worthy and powerful as that of fertile women.

The *Womb Healing – Female Energy Balancing* given by Moon Mothers can also help to support us on our journey towards completion. Moon Mothers work with the archetypal energy points within the body to release blocks and to restore energy to the archetypal aspects that are **already active** in our lives. This healing helps us to gently balance the flow of energy between archetypes and to merge them into the Complete Woman. *Womb Blessing Mentoring* offered by

Advanced Moon Mothers is particularly empowering for peri-menopausal and post-menopause women.

Menopause is not growing old – it is growing up

As Complete Women we are the ultimate expression of the human female. We can be Complete Women who are in the Enchantress phase of their lives, actively participating in the world as elders and mentors and women who build the future, or we can be Complete Women in the Crone phase of life who are outside of society, the keepers of spiritual wisdom, holders of stillness and guides to oneness.

Where the Maiden phase of life is a line, the Mother phase is a circle, the Enchantress phase is a spiral, **the final stage of female maturity is the single point of the Crone**.

Exercise: Energising your female energies – the Cauldron Breath

This breath works with the physical aspect of the womb centre (called the *Cauldron*) to help energy to flow into and within the centre. An energised womb centre helps peri-menopausal and post-menopause women to feel centred, strong, calm, complete and whole. It also helps their sexual energies to be awake and available to them.

The breath focuses on the three light archetypes of the female energies, the Maiden, Mother, and Enchantress. The fourth phase, the Crone, lies in the silent and still pause between the in and out breath.

> Take a small breath in, and as you do so tighten the muscles of your lower belly in a small contraction, drawing your lower belly slightly inwards. In your mind say 'Maiden'.

> Breathe in a little more, contracting the muscles of your lower belly a little more. In your mind say 'Mother'.

> Breathe in a little bit more, contracting the muscles of your lower belly even further, and say 'Enchantress'.

> Pause. In your mind say 'Crone'.

Breathe out, gently relaxing the lower belly in three stages.

We can do the Cauldron Breath several times in one session, and do it several times throughout the day. It is not necessary to do it in a special setting. This breath is a daily practice and the muscles of the lower body tighten as they get stronger.

Post-menopause women, women in peri-menopause and **pre-menstrual women** can find this breath very supportive and energising.

Completing the woman: Balancing the archetypes every day

As post-menopause women, all four archetypes are equally accessible to us. To help us bring our archetypes together to merge into completeness we can consciously connect to each one and deliberately express her energies during the day in small activities:

Maiden:
Accomplishing intellectual tasks and taking part in physical activity.
10 minutes / day doing accounts or going for a short walk.

Mother:
Focusing on the heart and sharing love through caring activities.
10 minutes / day gardening or making someone an unexpected cup of coffee.

Enchantress:
Undertaking creative projects and giving time to spiritual activities.
10 minutes / day writing a poem or colouring a mandala.

Crone:
Resting and listening for the heart's guidance.
10 minutes / day mindfulness meditation or just shutting your eyes.

When all four archetypes are deliberately expressed each day we begin to feel them as part of who we are. We also feel good because we are meeting our archetypal needs and expressing our authentic female nature.

Essential well-being for menopause:

We need 4 essential portions of the archetypes per day. One portion of Maiden, Mother, Enchantress, and Crone.
Are you getting your 4 a day?!

The world needs the beauty and wisdom of Complete Women

Every woman is unique, but we share many things in common. As we work with the archetypes we can share our experiences and the expressions of their energy, and in this way other women will also feel the resonance and call of their own inner archetypes. We can reach out to other women without a cycle and invite them to join the path of the Worldwide Womb Blessings to help them to awaken and embrace all aspects of their authentic femininity. We can help them to feel that their femininity is a gift, that the transformation to a Complete Woman is magical and empowering, and that the womb is more than just an organ but rather a sacred energy centre which encompasses our soul, our creativity and our spirituality.

The world needs the beauty and wisdom of Complete Women – women of depth and insight, magic and creativity – who are connected to the Sacred Feminine as her natural representatives.

The world needs women who are the white light as well as the rainbows.

Exercise: Embracing the Complete Woman – welcoming the gifts of her four faces

As well as being associated with the menstrual cycle, the stages of a woman's life, the moon and the seasons, the archetypes are also associated with the four directions. This daily ritual can help you to see the archetypes within yourself and to bring their gifts into your life.

Stand tall facing the east with your arms outstretched.

Say out loud: 'I have the clarity of a Maiden'

Face south and say: 'I have the love of a Mother'

Face west and say: 'I have the magic of an Enchantress'

Face north and say: 'I have the peace and calm of a Crone'.

Lift your arms above your head and say:

'I am all these things.

I am the whole of the cycle of the moon,
the whole of the cycle of the seasons,
the whole of the cycle of the life and
the whole of the cycle of the of the stars,
in one.'

Bring your hands to cross over your heart and say:

'I am woman complete within herself.'

Be aware that you are an amazing woman full of power, mystery, magic, and love.

Women without a cycle

Women without a cycle dancing with the moon

In menopause, when cyclic hormonal influences are no longer a factor, the influence of the moon's cycle can become more impactful and more important. Women who have always had a complex irregular cycle, or a cycle that has tended to be opposite to the archetypal energies of the lunar cycle (where they ovulate with the dark moon), finally have the chance to live in alignment with the archetypal energies of the moon. As these women journey into post-menopause they may be unaware of this change to lunar alignment, but if they consciously start to live within the rhythm of the moon, their inner female archetypes become more accessible to them and more balanced, bringing feelings of completeness.

The female archetype exercises in this book can be used in association with the moon's phases by **any woman without a cycle** – including post-menopause women, pregnant women, women on hormonal contraception, and women without a womb – and also by women with an erratic cycle, to **help them to nurture the changes and the awakening of the Womb Blessing attunement**.

All women without a cycle can live in harmony with the four female archetypes by dancing the cycle of the moon. This simply means living their lives by undertaking activities that resonate with the archetype of each lunar phase when the moon is in that particular phase.

Walking the moon's cycle: The Crone phase

3 days before the dark moon to 3 days after the dark moon

The Crone energies are strongest around the time of the dark moon, and then after a few days the energies change into the increasingly dynamic energies of the Maiden. Like a woman with a menstrual cycle, we rest during the darkness of the Crone energies and use this time to meditate, reflect, and feel connected to the oneness of the Universe. We move slowly, eat simply and allow time for inner guidance.

Walking the moon's cycle: The Maiden phase

3 days after the dark moon to 3 days before the full moon

The crescent moon appears in the sky between 1½ – 3½ days after the dark of the moon, depending on the orientation of the earth and sun, and then the Maiden energies start to flow. They begin slowly as they do in the menstrual cycle, and we can experience 'transition days' where we feel the energies from both the Crone and the Maiden archetypes within us. Following the light across the moon's face, we become increasingly active again in the world, doing exercise, starting projects, and learning new things. Like a woman in her pre-ovulation phase, we multi-task and take on the world with confidence!

Walking the moon's cycle: The Mother phase

3 days before the full moon to 3 days after the full moon

The Mother energies are strongest around the days of the full moon, and a few days after the full moon they start to change into the increasingly inner-world-focused energies of the Enchantress. Like the ovulation phase, this phase brings us energies of fullness, radiance, love and caring. It is a time for us to reach out to others, to offer support and caring and to show our gratitude and love. We move with sensual grace, touching others, content and whole.

Walking the moon's cycle: The Enchantress phase

3 days after the full moon to 3 days before the dark moon

The image of the decreasing crescent moon resonates deeply within us, and it is an image of magic and darkness. It heralds a time of increasing rest for us and of increasing spirituality, intuition and inspired creativity. Like a pre-menstrual woman, we have access to sexual sensuality, increasing inner stillness, and a desire to express our spirituality and creativity as it flows through us.

Maiden archetype	Mother archetype	Enchantress archetype	Crone archetype
Waxing moon	3 days before – 3 days after the full moon	Waning moon	3 days before – 3 days after the dark moon
Plan, take action and start projects	Show extra care and support for others	Give time to a creative or spiritual activity	Rest and reflect on the month and on the path ahead
Dance and be physically active	Connect with nature	Clear away the old	Nurture yourself and your body
Focus-based meditation (watching a candle)	Walking meditation (mindful of your senses and your experience of the world around you)	Visualisation meditation (visualising a scene and journeying through it)	Being-centred meditation (watching your breath)

Playful or flirty sexual acts	Romantic or sensual sexual acts	Adventurous or comforting sexual acts	Meditative or spiritual sexual acts

Women without a cycle dancing with the seasons

Some post-menopause women and women without a cycle can feel the changing seasonal energies more strongly than the lunar phase energies, and they can instead journey the path of the archetypes through the seasons to help them to understand, balance and express the archetypal energies within them.

Maiden archetype	Mother archetype	Enchantress archetype	Crone archetype
Spring	Summer	Autumn	Winter
The Earth Mother is young and flowering	The Earth Mother is sexual and gives birth	The Earth Mother clears the way and releases the seeds of future growth	The Earth Mother menstruates and rests
The land starts to awaken	The land is fertile and abundant	The land starts to sleep	The land rests and restores its energies
Start projects, be more active, have fun	Care for others, be practical and supportive	Clear space, use your intuition, be inspired and creative	Rest, listen to the wisdom in your soul

Living life to complete ourselves

As with all female archetypal energy work, it is important that we listen to our feelings and to our body and let them guide us in the unique relationship we have with the Sacred Feminine. But we also need to look up at night to see the moon's phase, we need to walk in nature to feel her energies, and we need to listen to our womb and to the call in our heart.

Chapter 9:
The Womb Blessing Path of female conscious living

'I am whole!' cried First Woman, and twirled around with her power objects on her belt.

She turned to Winter Old One and asked:

'So what do I do now?'

Winter Old One sucked hard on her pipe and smiled.

'Anything you want.' she said.

Between the Blessings: Living our authentic femininity

As we journey through each phase of our cycle after the Womb Blessing attunement, the energy releases restriction and opens our awareness to accepting more of each archetype. To support this process of awakening we can work consciously with the archetype of each phase to acknowledge her presence. We can discover her gifts and express her wonderful energies in our daily lives.

Walking the Path: A journey for all women

Why follow the Path?

The Womb Blessing Path is a series of activities aligned with the menstrual cycle, the lunar cycle, and the seasons to help women with or without a cycle to work consciously with the four archetypal energies.

The Path is designed to support the Womb Blessing attunement, but it can be used by any woman at any time.

The path helps **all women** to:

- Ground the energy changes made by the attunement in their body and in their life.

137

- Nurture and support their birthing into a new woman after the attunement.
- Embrace and celebrate the changes and healing during birthing.
- Build between Womb Blessings a loving, expressive and harmonious relationships with their womb centre, the archetypes and the Sacred Feminine.
- Stay connected to the archetypal energies throughout the month.
- Grow in confidence and empowerment between Blessings.
- Create a more balanced and harmonious cycle.

The Womb Blessing Path helps us to continue to grow in a loving dialogue between ourselves and our womb centre, the archetypes, and our cyclic nature.

**The Womb Blessing Path is about
supporting the changes made in
the Womb Blessing attunement,
continuing to grow and heal between Blessings,
and discovering
how we can feel love, joy, well-being and
fulfilment in every phase, each month.**

The keys to the Path

- Give yourself permission to be free to be who you are.
- Allow yourself to express who you are in each phase.
- Do one thing in each phase that is in harmony with the energies of your archetype.
- Everything will pass – so enjoy the gifts while you have them and know that any challenges will pass.
- The world does not yet make it easy for women to live female conscious lives, so be flexible and realistic.
- Be aware of your body, your way of thinking, your emotions and feelings – this is how you will recognise the archetypes within you.
- Create your own personal language and images for your archetypes.

Walking the Womb Blessing Path if you have a menstrual cycle

For the sake of simplicity, the Womb Blessing Path is 28 days long. 28 days is an *average cycle length*, which means that many women have a natural cycle that is longer or shorter than this.

If your cycle is longer or shorter you may be aware of your energies changing on days before or after the day outlined in the Path. Don't worry – the Path is a dance, so be flexible and adaptive and let your body and your intuition tell you what to do. If it feels right to skip ahead, then do the exercises from the next phase. If it feels good to repeat activities, then enjoy them again. If you find that you are drawn to activities in a completely different phase then do them if they feel good for you.

There are no rules for dancing this path with the Sacred Feminine – and only one guideline: if it feels good, this is your intuition showing you that the activity or thought is in tune with your cycle phase archetype.

Walking the Womb Blessing Path if you are without a cycle or have an erratic cycle

If you do not have a cycle or your cycle is very erratic, you can walk the path by undertaking the activities and suggestions during the lunar phase associated with each archetype – indicated at the top of each archetype section.

Women who are without a cycle due to pregnancy or breast-feeding may still be aware of an energy cycle within their body.

About the Focus Bowl exercise

When we first start to consciously journey along the path of our menstrual cycle it can be difficult for us to realise where we are going, where we have been and who we are. On the Womb Blessing Path we are going to use our womb bowls – the two bowls we use for the Worldwide Womb Blessings – to help us to see our changes.

You will need your two womb bowls and approximately 14 white stones and 14 dark stones. Wash the stones under a running tap, let them dry and place them all in one of your womb bowls. Every day this month you are going to pick out one stone from this bowl, either a dark stone or a light stone depending on your phase, and place it in the other womb bowl, which is now called your **Focus Bowl**.

The menstrual cycle is a journey from the outer world into the inner spiritual world and back out again. It is a daily path of changing dynamic and receptive energies reflected in the increasing and decreasing light of the moon. The black and white stones in our Focus Bowl will help us to recognise our gradual change as their number increases and decreases.

As you journey around the Womb Blessing Path and place your stones in your Focus Bowl you will become more aware of the beautiful flowing nature of your cycle and how you dance a path from light to dark to light.

The
Womb Blessing Path

Dark Moon Crone Phase, Cycle Days 1–6

**In the loving darkness
the Sacred Feminine gifts you the power
to renew your confidence and strength.
To receive it:
simply be.
Nothing in the outside world is this important.**

Based on 'Spiritual Messages for Women' by Miranda Gray

Cyclic women	Menstrual cycle	Menstrual phase: Approximately cycle day 1–6
Non-cyclic women	**Lunar cycle**	Dark moon: 3 days before the dark moon – 3 days after the dark moon
	Seasonal cycle	Winter

In the darkness we wait

Today we sit in the darkness at the centre of the labyrinth. Although this is cycle day 1, this is not the beginning of our energetic cycle – that comes with the spring, the new moon and the start of the pre-ovulation phase. For now, we wait, we rest and we enjoy the pleasure of our withdrawal from the world.

Cycle Day 1: The Crone's Bowl

You will need:

- one womb bowl – called the *Focus Bowl*.
- one womb bowl containing 14 white stones and 14 black stones, or more depending on the length of your cycle.

This **evening**, sit with your Focus Bowl on your lap.

Close your eyes and bring your awareness to your womb centre. See, know or feel that a beautiful cauldron lies in your pelvic girdle. Hold this image in your mind and be open to any experiences and feelings it brings.

If you are just starting the Womb Blessing Path, pick one dark stone and place it in the empty Focus Bowl.

If you are already on the Womb Blessing Path, notice how many dark stones there are in your Focus Bowl. See how the dark stones reflect your experiences of increasing withdrawal and increasing inner world energies over the Enchantress phase. You have journeyed from the light outer world to the heart of the labyrinth, and the comforting and embracing cave of your soul. Add a dark stone to your Focus Bowl and remove any remaining white stones if you have them.

As you place the dark stone in your Focus Bowl say:

> **From the increasing darkness I pause in the fullness of the dark.**
> **From the Enchantress I soften into the Dark Moon Crone.**
> **From the need to be wild I step into the need to 'be'.**

Keep your Focus Bowl resting in your lap and spend a few minutes feeling what this change means to you.

When you are ready to end, connect to the Earth Mother by imagining that you are growing roots from your Womb Tree deep into the earth.

Now place your bowls somewhere you will see them throughout the day.

Cycle Day 2: Opening to the Dark Moon Crone

Focus Bowl

This **evening,** sit with your Focus Bowl on your lap.

Bring your awareness to your womb centre and see, know or feel that a beautiful cauldron lies in your pelvic girdle. Hold this image in your mind and be open to any experiences and feelings it brings.

Place another dark stone in your Focus Bowl, in acknowledgement of your withdrawal, and say:

> **I open to the Dark Moon Crone.**
> **I welcome her energies of stillness, wisdom and love.**
> **I express her freely in my life.**
> **Tomorrow I will...**

Add a single activity or action that you will do tomorrow that will express your Dark Moon Crone energies and how you feel. If it is not obvious to you, spend a little time with your Focus Bowl resting in your lap and ask the Crone to inspire you. Remember, you can give yourself permission to do activities such as 'do nothing', or 'rest', or 'gaze out of the window'.

Connecting with your energies

Choose a piece of ribbon or thread in a colour that represents the Crone energies to you. This could be black, deep crimson, or midnight blue.

Tie the thread around your wrist and wear this bracelet throughout the phase as a positive statement of your Crone energies and as a reminder of who you are.

Cycle Day 3: The Dark Moon Crone and the Womb Blessing meditation

Focus Bowl

Start this **evening** by repeating the Focus Bowl exercise from Cycle Day 2.

Connecting with your energies

This **evening** do the Womb Blessing Meditation (the words are at the beginning of the book), taking your time to visualise each part of the meditation. In this phase you may find that you go deeper into the meditation and feel a greater sense of oneness, and that you are more aware of your connection to the Sacred Feminine.

- What did you feel or see during the meditation?
- What did you want to do after the meditation?

Note any insight or inner knowledge that comes into your mind over the next few days.

Cycle Day 4: Allowing the Dark Moon Crone sexual energies

Focus Bowl

Start this **evening** by repeating the Focus Bowl exercise from Cycle Day 2.

Connecting with your energies

For many women this phase is a sexless one. It can feel too messy, too embarrassing, or you have only the desire to sleep. Some women experience sexual desire, while others feel none at all.

The fatigue we feel in this phase doesn't have to stop sex, it just changes how we approach it. If we see ourselves not as tired but rather as held in the arms of the Crone energies we can focus on our sensuality and our spiritual awareness. Having slow and gentle sex – where our partner does the work – is a beautiful prayer to the Sacred Feminine. Whether we orgasm or not, whether we stay awake or not, doesn't matter – we have offered up a physical prayer to the Sacred Feminine through our body and our love for another.

Today notice the spiritual sensuality of the Dark Moon Crone sexual energies. See every touch as a caress, a sharing of spiritual love with the world around you.

If you have a partner, share your understanding of your sexual nature in this phase, and together experiment with where this takes your physical love.

You may find a difference between how you feel about sex at the beginning of the phase and later in the phase. Next month try this exercise on different days to discover your changing energies.

Cycle Day 5: Holding the Dark Moon Crone energies

Focus Bowl

Start this **evening** by repeating the Focus Bowl exercise from Cycle Day 2.

Connecting with your energies

The Crone is the Mother of the Cosmos and the Dark Mother of Souls. It is only our own fear of growing old and of death that prevents us from seeing her true nature of beauty and love.

Make time to step away from the world. Create a sanctuary of stillness and quiet to feel the Crone within you and to experience her wisdom and gifts of insight, restoration and oneness.

Sit or lie comfortably, close your eyes and take a deep breath.

Feel, know or see that you sit with your back against the trunk of a beautiful Womb Tree. Its roots grow deep into the earth and its branches reach up into a night sky that is filled with stars.

The sky above the branches of the tree is empty except for the darkness of space and the beauty of the stars.

Bring your awareness to your womb and womb centre, and feel or know that a large bowl sits resting in your pelvic girdle. The bowl is full of dark water.

Realise that it is the darkness that is always constant while the moon and your energies flow through their light phases.

Take a deep breath and relax. Open to the presence of the Dark Moon Crone within your womb centre and welcome her. Simply sit in her presence.

When you are ready to finish, thank the Sacred Feminine for her presence.

Bring your awareness back to your body and wiggle your fingers and toes. Take a deep breath. Stretch and smile.

It is okay to fall asleep in this meditation!

Use this meditation on different days, for example Cycle day 1 and Cycle day 6, to see how you change in this phase and what different types of wisdom are open to you.

Cycle Day 6: Healing the Dark Crone energies

Focus Bowl

Start this **evening** by repeating the Focus Bowl exercise from Cycle Day 2.

Connecting with your energies

Like the Full Moon Mother, the Dark Moon Crone is associated with deep love and compassion for all.

Sit comfortably and bring your awareness to your heart and be aware of the stars above your head.

As you gently breathe in, breathe the light of the stars down through your crown, through your heart and into your womb.

Stay relaxed and feel your womb filling with starlight and love.

In your mind say:

I am the Dark Mother.
I open to wisdom and soul healing.

When you feel ready to end the healing, place your hands over your lower belly and grow your Womb Tree roots deep into the earth.

Moving on to the next phase:

For some of us, our restoring rest at the centre of the labyrinth can continue for a few days after our bleeding has finished, while for others the Moon Maiden energies can start while we are still bleeding. Listen to your body and energies for the right time to reappear after hibernation rather than responding to the pressures and expectations of the world.

At the end of the phase you may like to thank the Sacred Feminine:

I thank the Sacred Feminine
for Her love,
for resting in my heart and in my womb
for the gifts She has given me
and for the passionate call to reclaim my authentic
femininity.

Dark Moon Crone phase summary:

What energies do you feel have been awakened for you by the Womb Blessing in this phase?

What aspects of your inner Dark Moon Crone do you feel have healed?

What insights or gifts has the Womb Blessing released into this phase for you to acknowledge and express?

If you received a Womb Blessing in this phase, what did you experience?

Moon Maiden Phase, Cycle Days 7–13

**In your phase of the waxing moon,
the energies are moving.
Can you feel this deep inside?
Go on – run with them!
Now!**

From 'Spiritual Messages for Women' by Miranda Gray

Cyclic women	Menstrual cycle	Pre-ovulation phase: Approximately cycle day 7–13
Non-cyclic women	Lunar cycle	Increasing moon: 3 days after the dark moon – 3 days before the full moon
	Seasonal cycle	Spring

From darkness into light

Today is the start of your pre-ovulation phase energies. After the hibernation of menstruation your energies have been renewed and restored, and now you start your journey from the cave of the Crone, or Dark Mother, out into the world. This is the true magic of being cyclic – that we can renew and restore our sexual, creative, mental, emotional and physical energies every month.

Today your new cycle starts!

Cycle Day 7: The Maiden's Bowl

The outward radiant energies of the Moon Maiden phase are growing and we are going to show this by adding a white stone to the Focus Bowl for each day of this phase and removing one black stone. You will have both white and dark stones in your Focus Bowl.

This **morning**, sit with your Focus Bowl on your lap.

Bring your awareness to your womb centre and see, know or feel that a beautiful cauldron rests in your pelvic girdle. Hold this image in your mind and be open to any experiences and feelings it brings.

Remove one black stone from your Focus Bowl and place it in the other bowl. Then place a white stone into your Focus Bowl.

If you are starting your Womb Blessing Path in this phase, simply add one white stone to your empty Focus Bowl.

As you add the white stone say:

> **From darkness I step into the light.**
> **From the Crone I step into the Maiden.**
> **From the inner world I step into the outer world.**

Spend a few minutes feeling what this change means to you.

When you are ready to end, connect to the Earth Mother by imagining that you are growing your Womb Tree roots deep into the earth.

As this phase continues you will see the number of black stones in your Focus Bowl decrease and the number of white stones grow, reflecting the increase of dynamic and outward energies in your womb as you walk through your Maiden phase.

Cycle Day 8: Opening to the Moon Maiden

Focus Bowl

In the **morning** repeat the exercise you did on Cycle Day 7, but this time as you remove a black stone and place the white stone in your Focus Bowl say:

> **I open to the Moon Maiden.**
> **I welcome her energies of beauty, of beginnings, and of delight and movement.**
> **I express her freely in my life.**
> **Today I will...**

Add a single activity or action that you will do today that will express your Maiden energies. For example; start a project, do some exercise, learn something new, do some planning or take time to do a task that needs concentration and attention to detail.

Connecting with your energies

Choose a piece of ribbon or thread in a colour that represents the Maiden energies to you. This could be white, yellow, pale pink, pale blue or light green.

Tie the thread around your wrist and wear this bracelet throughout the phase as a positive statement of your Maiden energies and as a reminder of who you are.

Cycle Day 9: The Moon Maiden and the Womb Blessing meditation

Focus Bowl

Start this **morning** by repeating the Focus Bowl exercise from Cycle Day 8.

Connecting with your energies

Today do the Womb Blessing Meditation (the words are at the beginning of the book), taking your time to visualise each part of the meditation. In this phase you may find it more difficult to sit still, but you may feel that you have more clarity and that it is easier to connect to the light.

- What did you feel or see during the meditation?
- What did you want to do after the meditation?

Note any thoughts, ideas or projects that come into your mind over the next few days.

Cycle Day 10: Holding the Moon Maiden energies

Focus Bowl

Start this **morning** by repeating the Focus Bowl exercise from Cycle Day 8.

Connecting with your energies

You are now well into the Maiden phase, and her energies are a large part of who you are. The following meditation is your opportunity to meet your inner Maiden and to allow her to show you her gifts.

Sit comfortably, close your eyes and take a deep breath.

Feel, know or see that you sit with your back against the trunk of a beautiful Womb Tree. Its roots grow deep into the earth and its branches reach up into a night sky that is filled with stars.

The crescent of the increasing moon lies cradled in the branches of the tree.

Bring your awareness to your womb and womb centre, and feel or know that a large bowl sits resting in your pelvic girdle. The bowl is full of dark water.

The moon bathes you in a gentle light that flows over you and down through your crown, through your heart and into your womb.

You see the crescent of the moon reflected in the waters of your bowl.

Take a deep breath and relax. Open to the presence of the Moon Maiden within your womb centre and welcome her.

When you are ready to finish, thank the Sacred Feminine for her presence.

Bring your awareness back to your body and wiggle your fingers and toes. Take a deep breath and stretch.

Make a note of any impressions or feelings your Maiden brought to you. How can you express her energies and presence in your life this week?

Cycle Day 11: Expressing your Moon Maiden

Focus Bowl

Start this **morning** by repeating the Focus Bowl exercise from Cycle Day 8. Your Focus Bowl will now have more white stones than black stones.

Connecting with your energies

As well as bringing us a different energy, each of the four archetypes also gives us a strong need to express this energy. Many women hold a lot of frustration in their bodies and in their cycles because they are restricted or limited in expressing the archetypal energy, or because they don't understand how to express it. By discovering the archetypal needs in each phase we can take action to fulfil these needs, and the result is that we feel happier and become more self-empowered. We reclaim control of what makes us feel good.

Sit comfortably and close your eyes.

Bring your awareness to your womb and womb centre.

As you breathe in, in your mind say:

I open my womb to the Moon Maiden.
Please come sit in my womb.

Relax on the out-breath.

Repeat for a minute.

See, know or feel that a beautiful young maiden is standing in front of you surrounded by a spring landscape.

She stands tall and confident, her hunting dogs at her feet, her silver bow and arrows on her back.

You feel her dynamic energy flowing through you, creating feelings of self-confidence and renewed sexual energy. Life feels full of new beginnings, goals, and the drive to achieve your dreams.

Now in your mind ask her:

What do I need to do to welcome and express your energy in my life?

Relax for just *one minute*.

Be open to receive any impressions or feelings or images. You may have a strong urge to do something simple, practical and everyday like looking for something you have lost, starting a new diet, signing up for the class you've always wanted to do, or planning your next holiday.

End the exercise by wiggling your fingers and toes and taking a deep breath.

Now take action! If it is impossible to completely meet your need, then do something small *towards* making it happen. Simply recognizing the Moon Maiden's need within you and taking a small action will make you feel less stressed, happier and more fulfilled.

Write down any inspiration or ideas to refer to in your next Maiden phase. Consciously connecting with her and expressing her energies in your life will not only help you to support the changes of the Womb Blessing and help you to embody your authentic female energies, but you will also feel good!

Cycle Day 12: Awakening the Moon Maiden sexual energies

Focus Bowl

Start this **morning** by repeating the Focus Bowl exercise from Cycle Day 8.

Connecting with your energies

Every phase of our cycle brings a different expression of sexual energy, and the Moon Maiden phase offers us a renewed sexual desire, whatever our age. The sexual energy of the Maiden is fun and playful, dynamic and self-assured, and given to us by nature for our own pleasure.

Today allow your Maiden sexuality the freedom to be expressed in the way you dress and the way you interact with people. Know or feel that whatever your age you have the sexual energies and beauty of the young Moon Maiden lying in your womb. Let her renewed beauty shine from your eyes, and smile with the mischievous and playful magic she brings.

If you have a partner, let them meet your Moon Maiden in the bedroom or wherever she desires!

Cycle Day 13: Healing the Moon Maiden

Focus Bowl

Start this **morning** by repeating the Focus Bowl exercise from Cycle Day 8. Your Focus Bowl will now contain seven white stones, showing that you have finally finished your climb from the darkness of menstruation out into the world.

Connecting with your energies

The Moon Maiden is associated with higher thoughts and ideals, and the Womb Blessing helps us to awaken and live this aspect of ourselves.

> Sit comfortably and bring your awareness to the energy centre that lies deep within your head.
>
> Be aware of a crescent moon above your head.

As you gently breathe in, breathe the white light of the Moon Maiden into your brain. Stay relaxed and feel your brain filling with light and clarity.

Say in your mind:

I am the Bright Maiden.
I open to beauty and healing purity.

When you are ready to end the healing, place your hands over your lower belly and grow your Womb Tree roots deep into the earth.

Moving on to the next phase

Depending on your cycle you may feel that your Moon Maiden phase has softened into the Full Moon Mother phase and that you are ready to move fully into her energies. However, if you feel that the Maiden energies are still strong you may want to repeat some of the Maiden activities for a few days until you feel the change to the next phase.

At the end of the phase you may like to thank the Sacred Feminine:

I thank the Sacred Feminine
for Her love,
for resting in my mind and in my womb
for the gifts She has given me
and for the passionate call to reclaim my authentic
femininity.

Moon Maiden phase summary

What energies do you feel have been awakened for you by the Womb Blessing in this phase?

What aspects of your inner Moon Maiden archetype have healed?

What insights or gifts has the Womb Blessing released into this phase for you to acknowledge and express?

If you received a Womb Blessing in this phase, what did you experience?

Full Moon Mother Phase: Cycle Days 14–20

Focus on today.
What will you do with love?
What opens your heart?
There is no need for anything else.

From 'Spiritual Messages for Women' by Miranda Gray

Cyclic women	Menstrual cycle	Ovulation phase: Approximately cycle day 14–20
Non-cyclic women	Lunar cycle	Full moon: 3 days before the full moon – 3 days after the full moon
	Seasonal cycle	Summer

In the light we shine

The dynamic energies have now slowed and our ego has softened in the radiant energy of the Full Moon Mother. Our energies are given to us to share with others, to create the world around us, and our heart is big enough to enfold the earth.

Cycle Day 14: The Full Moon Mother's Bowl

This **morning** sit with your Focus Bowl on your lap.

Bring your awareness to your womb centre and see, know or feel that a beautiful cauldron rests in your pelvic girdle. Hold this image in your mind and be open to any experiences and feelings it brings.

The outward radiant energies of the Full Moon Mother phase are strong, and we are going to show this by adding a white stone to the Focus Bowl for each day of this phase.

If you have any remaining black stones in your Focus Bowl, remove them.

If you are starting the Womb Blessing Path, simply add a white stone to your empty Focus Bowl.

As you put the white stone into your Focus Bowl say:

From the increasing light, I pause in the fullness of light. From the Moon Maiden I soften into the Full Moon Mother.
From the need to take action I step into the need to care.

Keep the bowl with the white stones resting in your lap and spend a few minutes feeling what this change means to you. When you are ready to finish, connect to the Earth Mother by imagining that you are growing roots from your Womb Tree deep into the earth.

Cycle Day 15: Opening to the Full Moon Mother

Focus Bowl

In the **morning** repeat the exercise you did on Cycle Day 14, but this time as you place the white stone in your Focus Bowl say:

I open to the Full Moon Mother.
I welcome her energies of empathy, of caring and of gentleness and love.
I express her freely in my life.
Today I will…

Add a single activity or action that you will do today that will express your Mother energies. For example: give your children extra hugs, call a friend you haven't spoken to recently, thank a work colleague for their recent help, bake cookies for your partner, or spend a little time gardening.

Connecting with your energies

Choose a piece of ribbon or thread in a colour that represents the Full Moon Mother energies to you. This could be white, deep pink, strong blue or emerald green.

Tie the thread around your wrist and wear this bracelet throughout the phase as a positive statement of your Mother energies and a reminder of who you are.

Cycle day 16: Full Moon Mother and the Womb Blessing meditation

Focus Bowl

Start this **morning** by repeating the Focus Bowl exercise from Cycle Day 15.

Connecting with your energies

Today do the Womb Blessing Meditation (the words are at the beginning of the book), taking your time to visualise each part of the meditation.

- What did you feel or see during the meditation?
- What did you want to do after the meditation?

Note any feelings and emotions you experience over the next few days.

Cycle Day 17: Holding the Full Moon Mother energies

Focus Bowl

Start this **morning** by repeating the Focus Bowl exercise from Cycle Day 15.

Connecting with your energies

For some women the change to the Mother phase can be difficult if they need the dynamic 'go-getting' energies of the Maiden for their work. For other women this phase can be deeply poignant and emotional because they want to be mothers, and the energies of this phase show them who they want to become.

Sit comfortably, close your eyes and take a deep breath.

> Feel, know or see that you sit with your back against the trunk of a beautiful Womb Tree. Its roots grow deep into the earth and its branches reach up into a night sky that is filled with stars.

> A beautiful radiant full moon lies cradled in the branches of the tree.

> Bring your awareness to your womb and womb centre and feel, or know, that a large bowl sits resting in your pelvic girdle. The bowl is full of dark water.

The full moon bathes you in abundant light that flows over you and down through your crown, through your heart and into your womb.

You see the face of the full moon reflected in the waters of your bowl.

Take a deep breath and relax. Open to the gentle, loving and calming presence of the Full Moon Mother and welcome her.

When you are ready to finish, thank the Sacred Feminine for her presence.

Bring your awareness back to your body and wiggle your fingers and toes. Take a deep breath and stretch.

Now draw or describe any feelings the Mother brought to you. How can you express her energies and presence in your life this week?

Cycle Day 18: Expressing your Full Moon Mother

Focus Bowl

Start this **morning** by repeating the Focus Bowl exercise from Cycle Day 15.

Connecting with your energies

Each phase of your cycle has different needs related to the archetypal energies. These needs are about living true to our authentic female nature, and when we meet a phase need it feels good! Pleasure shows us that we are in alignment with our authentic nature.

It is not enough to just recognize a need, we have to fulfil it for ourselves. Sometimes this is not possible, but amazingly just one small action taken towards meeting a phase need is often enough to create feelings of happiness and pleasure.

Sit comfortably and close your eyes.

Bring your awareness to your womb and womb centre.

As you breathe in, in your mind say:

**I open my womb to the Full Moon Mother.
Please come sit in my womb.**

Relax on the out-breath.

Repeat for a minute.

See, know or feel that in front of you sits a pregnant woman, surrounded by trees and summer flowers. She holds a basket full of bread, embroidered cloth and woven bowls.

She smiles at you, and you feel her contentment and fertility filling you with love, creativity, compassion, and caring.

Now in your mind ask her:

What do I need to do to welcome and express your energy in my life?

Relax for just one minute.

Be open to receive any impressions or feelings or images that she brings. You may have a strong urge to do something simple, practical and everyday like spending more time with your family, having a 'date' with your partner, doing crafts, listening longer to a friend's problems, or offering a little more of your time to help someone.

End the exercise by wiggling your fingers and toes and taking a deep breath.

Now take action! Write or draw any inspiration and ideas on how to meet these needs. Refer to your notes next month to help you to connect with the Full Moon Mother energies within you, express her energies and feel good!

Cycle Day 19: Embracing the Full Moon Mother sexual energies

Focus Bowl

Start this **morning** by repeating the Focus Bowl exercise from Cycle Day 15.

Connecting with your energies

For some women the Full Moon Mother phase can be a wonderful, passionate phase of heightened sexual desire. Nature gives us a higher desire for sex because we are releasing an egg and are fertile. But she also gives us enhanced feelings and emotions, so we are more likely to create an emotional attachment and commitment to our partner.

In the Mother phase we can feel more romantic, passionate and physically loving, as well as being able to connect with our partner at a deep emotional level.

Today, notice your Mother sexual energy and enjoy this loving, caring, romantic, passionate and sexy aspect of yourself. Know that whether you are a mother or not, you hold the enveloping, generous and abundant sexual energies of the Mother archetype within you. Let her sensuality and creative fullness flow from you today.

If you have a partner, how can you give the Mother what she wants in your existing relationship? Let your partner meet her!

Cycle Day 20: Healing the Full Moon Mother

Focus Bowl

Start this **morning** by repeating the Focus Bowl exercise from Cycle Day 15. Your Focus Bowl will now contain 14 white stones, showing that the Bright Mother phase is nearly over and then you will start your slow walk into the darkness again.

Connecting with your energies

The Full Moon Mother is associated with deep love and compassion for all.

> Sit comfortably and bring your awareness to your heart and be aware of a full moon above your head.
>
> As you gently breathe in, breathe the white light of the Full Moon Mother down through your crown and into your heart.
>
> Stay relaxed and feel your heart filling with light and love.
>
> In your mind say:
>
> **I am the Bright Mother.**
> **I open to love and emotional healing.**
>
> When you feel ready to end the healing, place your hands over your lower belly and grow your Womb Tree roots deep into the earth.

Moving on to the next phase

Depending on your cycle you may feel that you started to change into the Enchantress phase a few days ago, or you may feel that you are still deeply immersed in the Mother phase. If you are not yet ready to take the first steps into the Enchantress phase you can repeat some of the Mother phase activities until you do feel ready.

At the end of the phase you may like to thank the Sacred Feminine:

> **I thank the Sacred Feminine**
> **for Her love,**
> **for resting in my heart and in my womb**
> **for the gifts She has given me**
> **and for the passionate call to reclaim my authentic**
> **femininity.**

Full Moon Mother phase summary

What energies do you feel have been awakened for you by the Womb Blessing in this phase?

What aspects of your inner Full Moon Mother archetype have healed?

What insights or gifts has the Womb Blessing released into this phase for you to acknowledge and express?

If you received a Womb Blessing in this phase, what did you experience?

Moon Enchantress Phase, Cycle Days 14–21

Enjoy your steps into the darkness.
You are sexy.
You are magical.
You are an enchantress.
Enchant and bewitch!

From 'Spiritual Messages for Women' by Miranda Gray

Cyclic women	Menstrual cycle	Pre-menstrual phase: Approximately cycle day 21 – menstruation
Non-cyclic women	Lunar cycle	Decreasing moon: 3 days after the full moon – 3 days before the dark moon.
	Seasonal cycle	Autumn

Stepping into the darkness

Take a deep breath. Don't look back. Be brave. Place your foot on the first downward step of the labyrinth.

Don't worry. In the darkness the Enchantress will hold your hand and guide you as you leave the gentle radiant light of the Full Moon Mother. Feel the wild powers of the Enchantress growing in your mind and body.

Cycle Day 21: The Moon Enchantress' Bowl

This **evening**, sit with your Focus Bowl on your lap. You are going to start your journey into darkness, so you are going to do your meditation in the evening to acknowledge this.

Bring your awareness to your womb centre and see, know or feel that a beautiful cauldron rests in your pelvic girdle. Hold this image in your mind and be open to any experiences and feelings it brings.

Take out one white stone from your Focus Bowl and replace it with one dark stone.

If you are just starting the Womb Blessing Path, simply place one dark stone in your empty Focus Bowl.

As you place the dark stone in your Focus Bowl say:

From the radiant light, I step into the darkness.
From the Full Moon Mother I become the Enchantress of
the Darkening Moon.
From the outer world I step into the inner world.

Know that you are taking the first small step down into the labyrinth. Your subconscious and soul levels of awareness wait in the beautiful darkness, and the Enchantress will guide you and hold your hand. You will travel through the land of the subconscious that is filled with wildness, inspiration, sexual energy, creativity and magic to the land of the soul where you will rest in the arms of the Sacred Feminine. As the light recedes you may want to look back and long for the land of the Mother archetype – but everyone knows, from myths and legends, that you should never look back!

Keep the bowl with the stone resting in your lap and spend a few minutes feeling what this change means to you. Look at this single seed of darkness on the light-filled womb – do you welcome it or feel grief at what you will leave behind?

When you are ready to end, connect to the Earth Mother by imagining that you are growing roots from your Womb Tree deep into the earth.

Cycle Day 22: Opening to the Moon Enchantress

Focus Bowl

This **evening,** sit with your Focus Bowl on your lap.

The number of dark stones will slowly increase to reflect your descending path from the light of ovulation into the darkness of menstruation. It reminds you of the withdrawal of the energies of your body, your mind and emotions, and your return to deeper levels of awareness and understanding.

Bring your awareness to your womb centre and see, know or feel that a beautiful cauldron lies in your pelvic girdle. Hold this image in your mind and be open to any experiences and feelings it brings.

Replace a white stone in your Focus Bowl with a dark stone and say:

I open to the Moon Enchantress.
I welcome her energies of magic and passion, and of

**intuition and inspiration.
I express her freely in my life.
Tomorrow I will…**

Add a single activity or action that you will do tomorrow that will express your Moon Enchantress energies. For example: when you have energy – clear out a cupboard or the garden, do the washing and cleaning, or go for a walk and write a poem in your head. When you are low in energy – curl up and powernap, have a luxurious bath, read your oracle cards, doodle or colour-in mandalas, knit something, or let your imagination soar!

Connecting with your energies

Choose a piece of ribbon or thread in a colour that represents the Enchantress energies to you. This could be black, deep magical purple, or midnight blue.

Tie the thread around your wrist and wear this bracelet throughout the phase as a positive statement of your Moon Enchantress energies and a reminder of who you are.

Cycle Day 23: The Moon Enchantress and the Womb Blessing meditation

Focus Bowl

This **evening** repeat the Focus Bowl exercise from Cycle Day 22.

Connecting with your energies

This **evening** do the Womb Blessing Meditation (the words are at the beginning of the book), taking your time to visualise each part of the meditation.

- What did you feel or see during the meditation?
- What did you want to do after the meditation?

Note any thoughts, ideas or projects that come into your mind over the next few days.

Cycle day 24: Holding the Moon Enchantress energies

Focus Bowl

This **evening** repeat the Focus Bowl exercise from Cycle Day22.

Connecting with your energies

The Enchantress is a sorceress, and her energy and guidance can take many shapes and forms. She can be very powerful or very soft, very challenging and transformational, and very creative and spiritual. You might like to do this meditation several times during this phase to see what inspiration and magic she offers you.

Sit comfortably, close your eyes and take a deep breath.

> Feel, know or see that you sit with your back against the trunk of a beautiful Womb Tree. Its roots grow deep into the earth and its branches reach up into a night sky that is filled with stars.
>
> The crescent of the decreasing moon lies cradled in the branches of the tree.
>
> Bring your awareness to your womb and womb centre, and feel or know that a large bowl sits resting in your pelvic girdle. The bowl is full of dark water.
>
> The decreasing moon bathes you in a magical light that flows over you and down through your crown, through your heart and into your womb.
>
> You see the crescent of the moon reflected in the waters of your bowl.
>
> Take a deep breath and relax. Open to the presence of the Moon Enchantress within your womb centre and welcome her.
>
> When you are ready to finish, thank the Sacred Feminine for her presence.
>
> Bring your awareness back to your body and wiggle your fingers and toes. Take a deep breath and stretch.

Draw or dance the feelings and inspiration your Moon Enchantress brought to you.

Cycle day 25: Expressing your Moon Enchantress

Focus Bowl

This **evening** repeat the Focus Bowl exercise from Cycle Day 22.

Connecting with your energies

The Enchantress phase is often the most challenging, so it is important that we understand the needs of this phase and how to express the Enchantress energies to create feelings of happiness, empowerment and well-being.

Sit comfortably and close your eyes.

Bring your awareness to your womb and womb centre.

As you breathe in, in your mind say:

> **I open my womb to the Enchantress of the Darkening Moon.**
> **Please come sit in my womb.**

Relax on the out breath.

Repeat for a minute.

See, know or feel that you are surrounded by swirling leaves and an autumn landscape. In front of you stands a beautiful mature woman wearing a cloak of raven feathers and holding a silver sickle.

She fills you with dynamic energy, desire, inspired creativity, and a deep awareness of your inner darkness and magic.

Now in your mind ask her:

> **What do I need to do to welcome and express your energy in my life?**

Relax for just *one minute*.

Be open to receive any impressions or feelings or images. You may have a strong urge to do something magical like reading oracle cards, or to do something creative, or to retreat from the world and nurture yourself with something luxurious.

End the exercise by wiggling your fingers and toes and taking a deep breath.

Now take action! If it is not possible to completely meet your need, then do something small *towards* making it happen. Simply recognizing the need of the Moon Enchantress within you and taking a small action will make you feel less stressed, happier and more fulfilled.

Write down or draw any inspiration or ideas and keep them to refer to in your next Enchantress phase. Consciously connecting with her and expressing her energies in your life helps you to support the changes of the Womb Blessing, to balance your cycle and to ease you through the pre-menstrual phase challenges with love and elegance.

Cycle Day 26: Summoning the Moon Enchantress sexual energies

Focus Bowl

Start this **morning** by repeating the Focus Bowl exercise from Cycle Day 22. The number of dark stones are growing in the bowl, reminding you each day that you are withdrawing from the light and travelling deeper into the dark of the labyrinth.

Connecting with your energies

The Enchantress phase can be an amazing phase sexually. So often we focus on the challenging aspects of the pre-menstrual phase and ignore the pleasurable gifts it brings!

For many women the Enchantress phase can be the most erotic and adventurous. There can be days when we are less inhibited, more willing to try something new, and we can feel empowered with sexual confidence and desire. There can also be days where we feel more emotionally vulnerable and become needy of emotional reassurance. Sex can show us that our partner still loves us and reassure us that we are still desirable, and it can be a source of emotional comfort and stress release.

Today, notice your Enchantress sexual energies and accept them in whatever form they take. Allow her super-sexy energies to flow through you with alluring grace or, placing a shawl around your shoulders to comfort and protect your openness, express your deepening sensual withdrawal into the darkness.

If you have a partner, let them experience the erotic, uninhibited sexual energies; or curl up together and, in your vulnerability, let them see the beauty of the spiritual and sensual darkness within you.

If you find that at this stage of your phase you are too tired to think about sex and your sexual energies seem far away, you can either do this exercise earlier in your phase next month or do the Cycle Day 27 exercise to help awaken your energies.

Cycle Day 27: Healing the Enchantress of the Darkening Moon

Focus Bowl

Start this **evening** by repeating the Focus Bowl exercise from Cycle Day 22.

Connecting with your energies

If we are not nurturing and expressing the Enchantress energies, our womb energy centre, the Cauldron, can often become depleted in energy. We can draw energies into the Cauldron to bring healing to the Enchantress, which softens the more challenging messages she brings us in this phase.

> Close your eyes and bring your awareness to your lower belly and your womb or womb centre lying just below your navel.
>
> Imagine that you are drawing circles on your lower belly with your hand. Use your intuition to guide which way to draw the circle and how fast. After a few moments you may feel your womb responding.
>
> When you feel ready, bring your awareness to your right hip, and start 'drawing' imaginary circles over your hip.
>
> Then bring your awareness to your left hip and draw circles over it.
>
> Finally bring your awareness to your womb centre and see, feel or know that you are maintaining the energies swirling in all three locations.
>
> In your mind say:
>
> > **I am the Dark Maiden, the Enchantress of the Darkening Moon.**
> > **I open to magic and healing transformation.**
>
> When you feel ready to end the healing, place your hands over your lower belly and grow your Womb Tree roots deep into the earth.

Moving on to the next phase

Depending on your cycle you may feel that you became the Dark Moon Crone a few days before your bleeding, or you can still feel the Enchantress energies even though you are bleeding. If the Moon Enchantress energies are still strong you may want to repeat some of the Enchantress activities until you feel the change to Crone.

At the end of the phase you may like to thank the Sacred Feminine:

> **I thank the Sacred Feminine**
> **for Her love,**
> **for resting in my awareness and in my womb**
> **for the gifts She has given me**
> **and for the passionate call to reclaim my authentic**
> **femininity.**

Moon Enchantress phase summary

What energies do you feel have been awakened for you by the Womb Blessing in this phase?

What aspects of your inner Moon Enchantress archetype have healed?

What insights or gifts has the Womb Blessing released into this phase for you to acknowledge and express?

If you received a Womb Blessing in this phase, what did you experience?

The Womb Blessings and the Path

As we journey round our cycles, accepting and expressing the energies of the archetypes, we are accepting the energy changes and gifts that each Womb Blessing attunement offers us by making them part of ourselves and a part of our lives. At each Womb Blessing we step closer to our authentic nature and, even if modern life disconnects us, the Womb Blessing reconnects us and brings us back to who we are as women.

To walk the Womb Blessing Path in our lives is a step towards making things better – changing who we are and growing into a fuller version of our femininity. It brings us to a new place in our life, renewed and ready to bring love and female energies into the world.

Chapter 10:
The vision and the way forward

The Womb Blessing Vision

> First Woman lay on her blanket looking up at the stars. She was thinking about the first question she asked at the Making of the World:
>
> 'Who am I?'
>
> Now centred in her being, balanced and complete in her four power objects, and her womb bowl full of power, she knew the answer:
>
> 'I am me' she whispered to the Star People.

In societies where women are unaware of their authentic female nature, there are no authentic women to show them how to live and work in a way that is different to that of men. Behaving and thinking like men may bring material success, or safety and security, but it comes at a high price: guilt, emotional and mental disruptions, and stress and disharmony in the body and its cycles. So many women feel a deep and unfulfilled ache within – to understand who they are and to understand their purpose and path in life. They ache to feel whole, validated for who they are, and to feel confident and strong in their femininity and self-worth. But it only takes **one woman** to start living aspects of her authentic nature to begin to change the world.

When we connect with our authentic femininity and live it in the world, we naturally share our authenticity with other women and with our family. Women will resonate with our energies and with the way we live, and will want to know how they can also find this authenticity within themselves. Our children will see our authentic cyclic nature and how we live in harmony with it in the everyday world. Girls will have a role model for their own lives, and sons will understand the beauty, strength and worth in women's cyclic nature and learn how to dance with it.

As more and more women live and work in harmony with their female energies the benefits will become more obvious in their health, in their relationships, in their community and in their work. Authentic women will exhibit surprising skills and abilities. They will be insightful and creative, have wisdom beyond their years, understand intuitively, and live from a centre of peaceful empowerment.

The result will be change – but, rather than the battle of the sexes of the 1960s, this time change will be gentle. There will be a ground movement of women making small changes to their everyday lives that will shift the foundations of society. Old patterns of thinking will collapse, allowing a new and authentically female and authentically male society to co-evolve. The Womb Blessing is a way for women to start that change within themselves and within their own lives.

**The World is ready for change – and
that change will come from women.**

Sharing the vision

**The Womb Blessing Vision:
To create a harmonious world by awakening
all women to their authentic femininity.**

We aim to do this by providing all women with the opportunity to walk a path of female awakening through the Womb Blessing attunement and to give women the information they need to gain personal experience and understanding of their authentic female energies and nature.

Our heartfelt hope is to create a legacy for future generations so that our grand-daughters and their daughters grow up in a peaceful global society that acknowledges, teaches, celebrates and benefits from authentic femininity.

What if…?

What if we had a society that acknowledged the Cyclic Woman? One whose structure allowed women to be true to their cyclic nature?

What if medicine acknowledged the four phases, and tailored surgery and treatment to fit in with the cycle's energies? What if the effect of drugs took into account the phases of the menstrual cycle? What if there was a real will to understand the cycle and menopause?

What if mental health recognized the importance of adapting life to the four phases?

What if education allowed women and girls to learn in harmony with their cycles? To have continuous assessment, rather than exams, so that women can work and learn using the optimized skills of their phases?

What if there were a statutory Human Right that ensured recognition, support and education about the cyclic nature of women, and guaranteed the adoption of practices that make optimum use of women's full cyclic potential.

What if women were allowed one or two paid days off when menstrual, with time to catch up on tasks when their dynamic energies return?

What if women could work in a collaborative way, where they task-shared depending on the phase of their cycle and took roles in meetings and decision-making that reflected the different enhanced perceptive abilities of their phases?

What if the four creative and perceptive abilities of Cyclic Women were actively used in companies where these skills were used across departments, regardless of job titles?

What if menopausal women were respected as community leaders and business heads and were the major influence in politics and running countries?

What if we built a society where neither sex lives from their fear and survival patterns but lives instead from their authentic nature?

To change the world is a challenge – for many women it is dangerous and can be life-threatening, for others there is the threat that they would lose the worth and 'equality' that they have already fought hard to gain.

But,

what if …?

Afterword

First Woman danced her power.

Every day she looked for the face of Moon Mother in the sky and asked her for guidance and wisdom.

First Woman shared her life with the clans, living in tune with their rhythms. She brought the gifts she was given into the world, caring for the First Animals and using her creative energies to create a home and hearth. She used her sharp mind to organise and plan, and to learn the ways of the world. Her wild inspiration brought the magic and guidance of Spirit into the world, and her deep inner wisdom and intuition was sought by the First Animals as she sat by the fire and told stories.

Every activity was an expression of her powers, every activity connected her to her powers, and every activity was blessed by the light of the Moon Mother and the love of Mother Earth.

One day Moon Mother appeared to First Woman, and she took a little piece of the bowl that lay in First Woman's belly. She also took a little of the living water and creative flame that lay within it, and she took a little of the love from First Woman's heart.

Moon Mother mixed these items together in her own womb bowl and gave birth to First Man.

First Woman looked at him, pleased but puzzled.

'What does he do?' she asked.

'Dances with you' smiled Moon Mother.

And all was well.

There is no beginning or end, just the beautiful and eternal flow of seasons through which we women grow, blossom, fruit and rest.

As we journey through our cycles and the phases of our lives our relationship with the Sacred Feminine will change with the tempo of the music we dance to. How she appears to us, and how she guides us, will change. The archetypes we identify with will change, and our path in life will change. Awakened in our authentic femininity we gracefully dance our path, knowing that change is our strength and our nature as women and that we hold an intimate knowledge of it within our bodies. We also know that we hold the power to create with ease through surrendering to our cyclic nature and to heartfelt happiness.

Our nature is to be happy, loving and fulfilled.

Our path to this is to be who we truly are.

The Womb Blessing is a path of awakening our authentic nature guided by the Sacred Feminine. As She touches more and more women the Blessing will grow in many beautiful and diverse ways in response to the wonderful creativity and inspiration of women.

There are many paths ahead for us women to take, but the direction is the same.

You are invited to walk the path of the Womb Blessing with us.

The Sacred Feminine is within us,
around us,
and in every moment.
Nothing is bad, dirty or impure.
Everything is a sacred expression of Her.

Including you.

Exercise: A final exercise

While reading this book you will have absorbed the information through the filter of one or more archetypes – depending on how long it has taken you to read it. What you have thought and felt about the information, the conclusions you have reached and any action it has inspired, has been affected by the dominant archetype at the time of reading.

In my book *Red Moon* I suggest that readers re-read the information about a particular phase while in that phase, and there could be a few 'Aha!' moments for you if you do the same with this book.

When you re-read parts of the book, or do the exercises again, always be aware of the archetype you embody as you read.

For every piece of information, for every decision, for every activity, there are four approaches open to you. To be authentically feminine is to realise this and to use it as a positive force in your life.

Appendix

The Wheel of Year and the Archetype Meditations

The Worldwide Womb Blessings take place in the months of the major Celtic seasonal festivals – the dates of the festivals are given below. The Archetype Meditations are given for the Worldwide Womb Blessings in these months for both the southern and northern hemispheres.

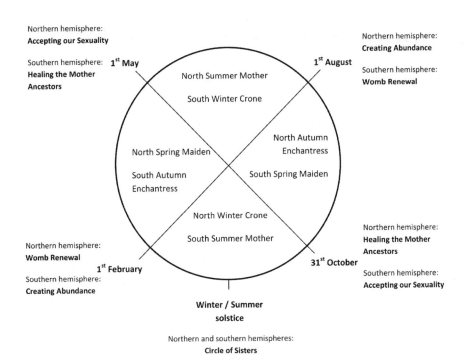

Northern hemisphere:
Accepting our Sexuality

Southern hemisphere: **1st May**
Healing the Mother Ancestors

Northern hemisphere:
Creating Abundance

Southern hemisphere:
Womb Renewal

1st August

North Summer Mother

South Winter Crone

North Spring Maiden

North Autumn Enchantress

South Autumn Enchantress

South Spring Maiden

North Winter Crone

South Summer Mother

Northern hemisphere:
Womb Renewal

1st February

Southern hemisphere:
Creating Abundance

Northern hemisphere:
Healing the Mother Ancestors

31st October

Southern hemisphere:
Accepting our Sexuality

Winter / Summer solstice

Northern and southern hemispheres:
Circle of Sisters

What to do at your chosen time on Womb Blessing day

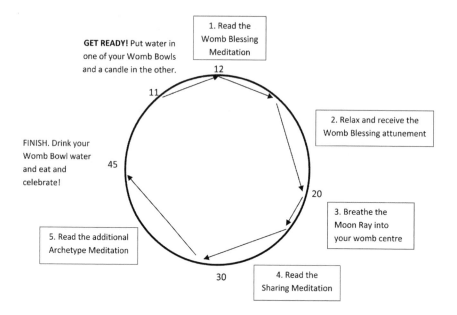

GET READY! Put water in one of your Womb Bowls and a candle in the other.

1. Read the Womb Blessing Meditation

12

11

2. Relax and receive the Womb Blessing attunement

FINISH. Drink your Womb Bowl water and eat and celebrate!

45

20

3. Breathe the Moon Ray into your womb centre

5. Read the additional Archetype Meditation

30

4. Read the Sharing Meditation

The Cycles of the Sacred Feminine.

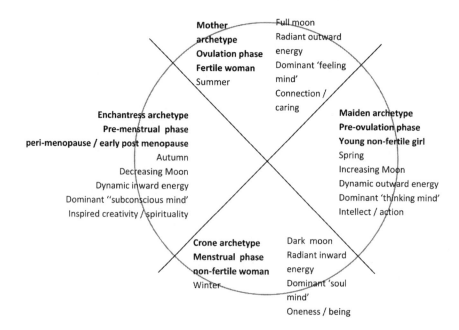

Mother archetype
Ovulation phase
Fertile woman
Summer

Full moon
Radiant outward energy
Dominant 'feeling mind'
Connection / caring

Enchantress archetype
Pre-menstrual phase
peri-menopause / early post menopause
Autumn
Decreasing Moon
Dynamic inward energy
Dominant "subconscious mind'
Inspired creativity / spirituality

Maiden archetype
Pre-ovulation phase
Young non-fertile girl
Spring
Increasing Moon
Dynamic outward energy
Dominant 'thinking mind'
Intellect / action

Crone archetype
Menstrual phase
non-fertile woman
Winter

Dark moon
Radiant inward energy
Dominant 'soul mind'
Oneness / being

How can I find a Moon Mother?

Moon Mothers are women who hold the Womb Blessing vibration of Sacred Feminine love and light and who are trained in Miranda's techniques to give both *Personal Womb Blessing* attunements and *Womb Healing - Female Energy Balancing* and to take an active role in the Worldwide Womb Blessing attunement. *Level 2 Moon Mothers* are trained in *The Gift* for men as well as expanded healing techniques, and *Advanced Moon Mothers* have received an additional training day in Womb Blessing Mentoring to companion women during their awakening.

Moon Mothers can help to answer questions about the Worldwide Womb Blessing, and many run Worldwide Womb Blessing groups – and they can help you to create your own group or find one in your area.

To see a list of Authorized Moon Mothers in your country visit www.wombblessing.com.

How can I become a Moon Mother?

The following training workshops are available in a number of locations worldwide.

The Moon Mother Practitioner Training workshop:

An intensive energy-working and information-full two-day training to raise women's vibration to that of a Moon Mother and to empower them to transfer the Womb Blessing energy in the *Personal Womb Blessing attunement*, the *Womb Healing – Female Energy Balancing* and in the Worldwide Womb Blessing. This is a practitioner workshop including supporting manual and online resources, certification and international listing.

Advanced Training

Level 2 Moon Mother workshop:

In this intense and information-rich one-day practical workshop Moon Mothers receive a beautiful initiation to increase the amount and vibration of the energy they can transfer in the Womb Blessing, and learn advanced female-energy-specific healing techniques to help their own awakening and healing and that of their Receivers. Includes *The*

Gift for men, *Female Soul Healing* and a *Self-Blessing*. The workshop includes supporting manual and international listing.

Advanced Moon Mother Mentor Training:

This intensive workshop is for Moon Mothers who are Level 2 or above, who wish to offer deeper support to their Receivers. By co-creating a personalised monthly programme, Advanced Moon Mothers help Receivers to support their healing and awakening by living a more authentic everyday life between Blessings. The workshop includes an initiation to open Moon Mothers to mentoring, a supporting manual, certification and international listing.

You can find a calendar of training workshops on www.wombblessing.com.

Cycle Training

Red Moon workshop:

An interactive introduction to the four female archetypes and their effects on our lives, with lots of information, practical group exercises and a unique group healing of the archetypes. This workshop is ideal for every woman with or without a cycle, and highly recommended for all Moon Mothers.

Credits

I would like to thank…

There is the most amazing team of women behind the Worldwide Womb Blessing.

It is not possible to individually thank all the women who help spread the Womb Blessing around the world, or who run Blessing groups and online groups. It is also not possible to thank all the individual Moon Mothers, Moon Mother Representatives and Country Co-ordinators and Co-ordination Teams for the voluntary work they do in supporting the Womb Blessing community. There are also all the organisers of the Womb Blessing workshops, the volunteer translators for workshops, manuals and newsletters and online information, the designers and web-developers. Without these women's help the Womb Blessing would not happen in this most amazing and exciting organic unfolding – and there are also the wonderful men who support us in our heartfelt service to change the lives of women and men for the better.

So 'thank you' to everyone in the Womb Blessing community for your amazing passion and skills, your creativity and love, and for your courage and inspiration and heartfelt commitment.

I would finally like to mention one person for special thanks – my husband Richard. Without his love and constant support and help, I would not be able to do what I do and we would not have a Worldwide Womb Blessing or a growing global community of women and Moon Mothers. My love and my heart have always been and always will be, yours.

Cover artwork by Liana Moisescu

My thanks to Deborah Willimott for her editorial input, ideas and help.

Also by Miranda Gray:

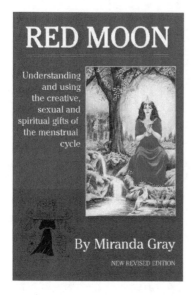

Red Moon: Understanding and using the creative, sexual and spiritual gifts of the menstrual cycle.

For our ancestors the menstrual cycle was a source of wonderful creative, spiritual, sexual, emotional, mental and physical energies. It was a gift that empowered women to renew themselves each month, to manifest and create the world around them, to connect deeply with the land and their family, and to express deep wisdom and inspiration. This ancient female teaching is still available to us in our mythology and nursery tales.

Miranda Gray introduces modern women to their unique cyclic nature and guides them in accepting and expressing a passionate and creative cycle-empowered life. She explores the women's wisdom contained in western mythology and traditional stories and offers practical exercises and methods (including the 'Moon Dial') to explore the depths of being a Cyclic Woman.

The Optimized Woman: Using your menstrual cycle to achieve success and fulfilment.

This book is for the 21st-century woman who wants to create well-being, fulfilment, work success, goal-achievement and the life she wants using a uniquely female approach.

Miranda Gray answers the question 'What use is my menstrual cycle?' by returning the cycle to its rightful place as a powerhouse of practical resources for women. The little-recognised secret lies in *Optimum Times* – days of enhanced abilities.

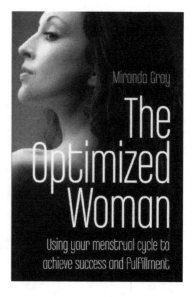

The book offers you a daily plan of Optimum Time practical activities that you can tailor to your circumstances and cycle – whether natural or medically managed. It helps you to identify and achieve your goals, increase excellence, build better relationships, create the ideal work/life balance, and generate personal happiness.

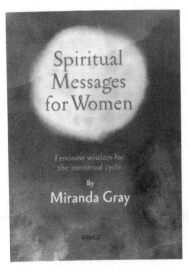

Spiritual Messages for Women: Feminine wisdom for the menstrual cycle

Does your heart cry out for a daily spiritual relationship with the Divine, but it just seems so difficult to hold on to? There is a secret female-only spiritual path.

Spiritual Messages for Women offers daily inspirational, supportive and loving guidance in tune with your four cycle phases, showing you how to create and enjoy a wonderful loving relationship with the Divine every day throughout the whole month.

Dip into the sections once a day or throughout the day to reach out to the Divine and join Her dance.

See www.mirandagray.co.uk for more information about Miranda's work and titles.